CANADA'S WORLD WONDERS

CANADA'S WORLD WONDERS

RON BROWN

DUNDURN
TORONTO

Cover image: Percé Rock, Quebec. Courtesy of the author.
Printer: Friesens

Library and Archives Canada Cataloguing in Publication

Brown, Ron, 1945-, author
       Canada's world wonders / Ron Brown.

Issued in print and electronic formats.
ISBN 978-1-4597-4094-5 (softcover).--ISBN 978-1-4597-4095-2 (PDF).--ISBN 978-1-4597-4096-9 (EPUB)

       1. Curiosities and wonders--Canada--Guidebooks. 2. Canada--Description and travel. 3. Canada--Guidebooks. 4. Guidebooks. I. Title.

FC38.B76 2018   917.104'74   C2018-903171-9
                                                      C2018-903172-7

1   2   3   4   5   22   21   20   19   18

We acknowledge the support of the **Canada Council for the Arts**, which last year invested $153 million to bring the arts to Canadians throughout the country, and the **Ontario Arts Council** for our publishing program. We also acknowledge the financial support of the **Government of Ontario**, through the **Ontario Book Publishing Tax Credit** and the **Ontario Media Development Corporation**, and the **Government of Canada**.

Nous remercions le **Conseil des arts du Canada** de son soutien. L'an dernier, le Conseil a investi 153 millions de dollars pour mettre de l'art dans la vie des Canadiennes et des Canadiens de tout le pays.

Care has been taken to trace the ownership of copyright material used in this book. The author and the publisher welcome any information enabling them to rectify any references or credits in subsequent editions.
                                                    — *J. Kirk Howard, President*

VISIT US AT

dundurn.com | @dundurnpress | dundurnpress | dundurnpress

Dundurn
3 Church Street, Suite 500
Toronto, Ontario, Canada
M5E 1M2

CONTENTS

Yukon, Canada.

CANADA'S WORLD WONDERS: WHAT ARE THEY?

Canada is blessed to have many natural and historic features that resonate around the world. While not all will have a UNESCO or even a national designation, they nonetheless attract the interest of those both inside and outside the country. Visitors journey from around the world to hike them, bike them, sail them, drive them, photograph them, or film movies at them.

Most of the entries in this volume, however, do find themselves on the world's lists of wondrous sights and adventures. Many are one of a kind, the largest of their kind, or simply a curiosity.

How many, even within Canada, know what a pingo is, or an inuksuk? Or that Alberta is recognized around the world as having a leading treasure trove of dinosaur fossils, some even intact, and has the world's leading museum to house them? Or that the world's oldest operating oil field lies not in Alberta or even the Middle East but in southern Ontario.

Much of Canada's world legacy lies in famous and infamous events that at one time attracted the world's attention, such as the frantic stampede to the Klondike goldfields and Franklin's ill-fated search for the Northwest Passage. While such events have faded into history, their visible legacy often survives.

Canada is a young country with an Indigenous heritage that long predates Confederation and the European invasions before that. The Haida Gwaii totems and Head-Smashed-In Buffalo Jump are unique in the world. While this human heritage may not rank with the pyramids of Egypt or the Taj Mahal, it has attracted the world's attention and often spawned a dynamic tourism industry. Natural features extend from the oddities in the Far North, such as the "burning hills," to the world's last temperate rainforests of the B.C. coast and the geological legacy of massive meteor craters.

It is not solely about tourist dollars, however, for many of the entries in this volume may be remote or hard to access. Rather, it is about a heritage, both natural and cultural, that allows Canada to stand out amid the world's wonders.

Prince Edward Island National Park.

ONE

CANADA ON THE WORLD STAGE

CANADA'S NATIONAL PARKS

Canada was one of the first nations in the world to create a system of national parks. The first such park was the result of lobbying not from any naturalist organization or civic-minded individuals but rather from a profit-motivated private railway company.

By 1886 the Canadian Pacific Railway, the "national dream" of Prime Minister John A. Macdonald, was running its first trains from Montreal into the Vancouver railway station. Its route carried it into the Rocky Mountains by way of the Kicking Horse Pass, through which flowed the Bow River. As the line was being surveyed, a trio of railway employees happened upon a pool of hot springs. With an eye to profit, the CPR's general manager, one William Cornelius Van Horne, acquired the site.

Entranced by the natural beauty of the ragged, snow-capped mountains, Van Horne also recognized the potential of the route to augment the railway's profits, claiming, "If we can't export the scenery, we'll import the tourists." But, to do that, he needed to ensure that this natural wilderness would remain unmarred.

In 1886 Van Horne began lobbying the federal government to preserve the hot springs and the surrounding area. In 1887 Macdonald's government acquiesced and created Rocky Mountains Park, later renamed Banff National Park. Yoho and Glacier National Parks, both along the railway line, soon followed. Within a few years, Canada's new system of national parks included Elk Island, Revelstoke, and Waterton.

In 1911 James B. Harkin became commissioner of Canada's national parks and established a rationale for their creation, namely to protect key natural features and make them relevant to Canadians. He addressed wildlife protection with Wood Buffalo National Park, in what was then the Northwest Territories, and a migratory bird sanctuary at Point Pelee on Lake Erie.

Harkin's overriding aim was to ensure that each province would have at least one national park, and he added parks in Saskatchewan at Prince Albert, Riding Mountain in Manitoba, Cape Breton Highlands in Nova Scotia, and the Thousand Islands and Georgian Bay Islands in Ontario. In 1930 parliament passed the National Parks Act to leave the parks "unimpaired for the enjoyment of future generations."

Banff poster. As soon as the Canadian Pacific Railway completed its cross-country line, it began promoting the Rocky Mountains with colourful posters.

Park creation lagged following Harkin's retirement and remained so until Jean Chrétien became minister of Northern Affairs and renewed the parks program. His aim was decidedly more for environmental protection and the representation of Canada's many natural landscapes. This led to the establishment of wilderness parks, such as La Mauricie and Forillon in Quebec, the Pacific Rim in British Columbia, Gros Morne in Newfoundland and Labrador, Pukaskwa in Ontario, and Nahanni and Kluane in northern Canada. The country's first national urban park was established in 2015 along the watershed of Toronto's Rouge River, protecting forests, farmlands, and riverine and wetland habitats. The Rouge National Urban Park, at 79.1 square kilometres, is the largest and best-protected national urban park in the world.

Other river systems also benefit from their designation as heritage rivers. In 1984 the federal government created an agency to designate Canada's heritage rivers. The designation process falls under the authority of Parks Canada. Submissions must go before the Canadian Heritage Rivers Secretariat (CHRS), where all provinces and territories have seats. Those nominations must support the river's value as a natural or heritage river.

Once designated, the implementation falls to river managers, which may range from provincial parks agencies to nonprofit groups. Although there are no federal legislative restrictions on the rivers or their shorelines, identifiable benefits include tourism, water management, public awareness, and improved river health. To date, forty-two rivers are part of the system, covering twelve thousand kilometres of river. Ontario leads the way with twelve rivers, while the province of Quebec does not participate. Among Canada's heritage rivers, Ontario's Rideau Waterway and the Northwest Territories' South Nahanni River are also UNESCO World Heritage Sites. The CHRS maintains a website (CHRS.ca) that describes the designation process and the rivers on their list.

Canada also enjoys a widespread system of provincial parks, most of which exist for recreational purposes. One of Canada's first provincial parks was Algonquin Provincial Park, created in 1893 as a national park. Then, following the creation of Canada's national parks system, Algonquin became a provincial park in 1913. The first railway arrived in 1895 and another later in 1913; they were used not just for hauling out logs but also for bringing in the tourists. The tracks are gone now, as are the little logging towns that lined them, with Brent, Kiosk, and Canoe Lake turning into ghost towns.

The park's original intent was to manage logging for the forest industry, but with its 2,400 lakes, it soon became popular with tourists and artists and attained recognition as a National Historic Site in 1992. The designation was primarily for its management and interpretative practices as well as for its history of inspiring such artists as Tom Thomson, who was killed in the park in 1917 while canoeing on Canoe Lake. Despite its international reputation as a wilderness destination, the main role of the park remains to serve the logging industry — Ontario's only provincial park to do so. A fine logging museum provides a self-guided trail that features displays of how logging evolved in the park, including an example of the curiously named "alligator" logging boat.

Confusion may arise in those choosing park destinations in Quebec, as that province also identifies its own provincial parks as "national" parks.

Today Canada's national parks number forty-seven, along with five national marine conservation areas and one national landmark. Six of these areas have the distinction of being UNESCO World Heritage Sites as well.

In a program created by Parks Canada in 2017 to celebrate Canada's 150th anniversary, red chairs were placed in national parks across the country to encourage Canadians to appreciate the beauty of the parks. These red chairs are located at Two Jack Lake in Banff National Park. Mount Rundle is in the background.

THE STORY OF CANADA'S NATIONAL HISTORIC SITES

Canada boasts an incredible 970 sites designated for their national historic significance. These include massive sites, such as the Fortress of Louisbourg reconstruction in Cape Breton, as well as roadside plaques that commemorate an individual or an event relevant to that spot. Those attractions considered more significant number 171 and are administered by Parks Canada. They include forts, lighthouses, historic buildings, battlegrounds, railway stations, and historic landscapes.

Sites across the country are chosen by the Historic Sites and Monuments Board of Canada. In addition the board has created the Canadian Register of Historic Places (CRHP), which contains relevant information about historic locations and structures selected for the register. Launched in May 2004, the CRHP is an online collaboration between the provinces and the federal government. To date, more than fifteen thousand structures, landscapes, and archaeological sites are in the searchable database.

Parks Canada also administers the Heritage Railway Station Protection Act, passed in 1988, and the Heritage Lighthouses Protection Act, passed in 2008, both pieces of legislation that came only after the threats to these historic structures resulted in many unnecessary demolitions.

Canada's heritage preservation efforts began in the late nineteenth century. Inspired by earlier efforts in France and the United Kingdom to protect sites of historic interest, in Canada, Governor General Lord Dufferin first proposed protecting the Fortifications of Quebec, which were then under threat of demolition.

In 1887 the government, at the instigation of the Canadian Pacific Railway (CPR), designated the Banff hot springs and the surrounding mountains as the Rocky Mountains Park. Then, in the early years of the twentieth century, the government began looking to extend the national parks system to eastern Canada and decided to add to it the region's many historic sites. In 1914 Fort Howe in Saint John, New Brunswick, became Canada's first national historic park, followed in 1917 by Fort Anne in Annapolis Royal, Nova Scotia. Two years later the government established the Advisory Board for Historic Site Preservation, the precursor to the National Historic Sites and Monuments Board (NHSMB). The first site that the new agency designated was the now largely forgotten Cliff Site in Port Dover, Ontario, the location of a cabin erected by two French priests in 1670, where they claimed French sovereignty over Lake Erie.

Prioritizing Canada's military glories, the NHSMB's early historic designations were for battles and prominent individuals, particularly those related to the War of 1812 and the United Empire Loyalists. Adhering to the country's decidedly white and Protestant biases of the day, the board deliberately omitted any historic locations related to blacks, Jews, Ukrainians, or Indigenous Peoples.

In the 1930s outside agencies started using Depression-era funding to restore historic structures, such as Kingston's Fort Henry, which was

The Hartland covered bridge, which crosses the Saint John River between Hartland and Somerville in New Brunswick, is the world's longest covered bridge, stretching just over 390 metres.

being restored by the Department of Highways, while the Niagara Parks Commission was restoring Fort George in Niagara-on-the-Lake.

In 1955 the National Historic Sites and Monuments Act broadened its own mandate to include historic buildings and structures. In the ensuing decades, it designated features of wider significance, such as Dawson City in Yukon, Fortress of Louisbourg on Cape Breton Island, and the Fortifications of Quebec City. Eventually, the board came around to also commemorating the many Indigenous Peoples and ethnic groups rejected by earlier boards.

By 2017 the board had identified more than 1,500 sites, with 268 in Ontario and 194 in Quebec. The other provinces and territories share the rest, while two sites in France are designated: the memorial at Beaumont-Hamel, where the Royal Newfoundland Regiment was virtually wiped out at the Battle of the Somme in 1916, unveiled in 1925, and the massive monument unveiled in 1936 on Vimy Ridge to commemorate the many dead soldiers who lie in unmarked graves.

Eighteen of Canada's National Historic Sites are included on UNESCO's list of World Heritage Sites. Six more sites, all pertaining to the heritage of Indigenous Peoples and located in western and northern Canada, remain on Canada's tentative list of proposed UNESCO sites.

UNESCO IN CANADA

In the late fall of 1972, members of the United Nations Educational Scientific and Cultural Organization (UNESCO) met in convention to discuss the increasing threats to the world's natural and cultural heritage, not just through vandalism, neglect, or through natural causes, like erosion or decay, but, more significantly, through the social and economic conditions that exacerbated their decline. The convention agreed that "in view of the magnitude and gravity of the new dangers threatening them, it is incumbent on the international community as a whole to participate in the protection of the [world's] cultural and natural heritage."

The convention went on to define "cultural heritage" as including monuments, groups of buildings, and sites considered to be of "outstanding universal value." It defined "natural features" as those geological

Built in 1900 by the CPR, McAdam Station, which combined a railway station and a luxury hotel, was built in the chateau style favoured by the CPR for its stations and hotels at the time. No longer in use as a station, today the restored structure functions as a museum and community facility and is a National Historic Site.

formations or natural habitats that are of "outstanding universal value" from an aesthetic, scientific, or conservation point of view.

It was, however, left up to each member state to identify and justify candidate sites or areas as well as plans to protect such sites. Those submissions would then be evaluated by a World Heritage Committee consisting of fifteen of UNESCO's member states, a process that could take several years.

The convention felt that it was not up to UNESCO to then impose a regulatory framework on them. Those measures were left to each member state and may include anything from the establishment of national parks to local planning controls. This way, local authorities are more active in establishing planning and regulatory controls around them, as has been done in Old Quebec City and Old Town Lunenburg. Other controls may have already been in place in such protected zones as national parks (e.g., Nahanni and Rocky Mountains) or national heritage attractions (Fortress of Louisbourg and Grand Pré).

To help fund studies by member nations in carrying out the protection of those sites, the convention went on to create the World Heritage Fund. Further, the World Heritage Committee has also created a list of fifty-four World Heritage in Danger sites (none of which are located in Canada) to alert the world to the threats facing them.

Among the first sites in Canada to gain UNESCO recognition were the L'Anse aux Meadows Viking archaeological site in Newfoundland and Labrador, Dinosaur Provincial Park in Alberta, and Nahanni National Park Reserve in northern Canada. To date, Canada can claim eight UNESCO cultural heritage sites and ten natural heritage sites.

In 2017 the Canadian government submitted six additional candidate sites for UNESCO's consideration. These are all related to the heritage of Indigenous Peoples and are situated in either western or northern Canada. The Fairbank oil field in southwest Ontario, which is one of the world's oldest operating oil fields and uses hundred-year-old technology, is currently under consideration by the government as a tentative site.

UNESCO has also established a registry of World Biosphere Reserves. Biosphere reserves are areas comprising terrestrial, marine, and coastal ecosystems where the goal is to promote solutions reconciling the conservation of biodiversity with sustainable use. As with World Heritage Sites, biosphere nominations are submitted for consideration by the various member states. At present there are 669 such reserves in 120 countries. While such reserves may lack the visual prominence of heritage sites, they are nonetheless important for recognizing significant natural areas and encouraging education and sustainable development.

Biosphere reserves consist of three zones: (1) a core area that comprises a strictly protected ecosystem that contributes to the conservation of landscapes, ecosystems, species, and genetic variation; (2) a buffer zone that surrounds or adjoins the core areas and is used for activities compatible with sound ecological practices; and (3) a transition zone around that buffer where sustainable development is to be encouraged. Nominees are submitted by the member nations to the Advisory Committee on Biosphere Reserves, which then forwards its recommendations to the International Coordinating Committee for a final decision. This process can take up to a year.

At present Canada hosts eighteen biosphere reserves. The first to gain recognition was Mont-Saint-Hilaire in Quebec, achieved in 1978, followed by Waterton, Alberta, in 1979. Few of Canada's biosphere reserves are immediately recognizable, as most lack fences, gates, or, in most cases, "you are entering" signs. Most, however, are promoted within their respective regions. Included in this work are Charlevoix in Quebec, and the Niagara Escarpment, Frontenac Arch, and Georgian Bay Islands, all in Ontario.

UNESCO lacks the mandate to regulate uses within the reserves. Rather, it is up to provincial and municipal authorities to determine how best to manage them. Even then, few local authorities impose regulatory control but rather use their designation as an educational opportunity to encourage sustainable management. Some, such as the Frontenac Arch Biosphere Reserve near Gananoque in Ontario, have opened a special office that offers brochures on the aims of the reserve and the various sites within it. In that sense, the designation becomes as much a branding exercise as an educational one.

With their designation of World Heritage Sites and World Biosphere Reserves, UNESCO has brought the world's attention to many of Canada's intriguing natural and historic wonders.

In a CBC competition, audience members and a panel of judges voted for Canada's "Seven Wonders."

The judges chose:

- the canoe
- Pier 21
- Niagara Falls
- Prairie skies
- the igloo
- Old Quebec City
- the Canadian Rockies

The public selected:

- the Bay of Fundy
- Nahanni National Park
- the Northern Lights
- the Canadian Rockies
- the Cabot Trail
- Niagara Falls
- the Sleeping Giant

In July 2018, UNESCO announced Canada's first mixed designation, combining both natural and cultural attributes. At nearly thirty thousand square kilometres, Pimachiowin Aki is also one of Canada's largest UNESCO designations. In the works since 2012, it encompasses a vast region on the Manitoba and Ontario border, northeast of Winnipeg. The region includes extensive boreal forests, one of Canada's largest caribou herds, and four Indigenous nations. It is only the second such designation in North America, the other being in Mexico.

TWO

THEY CAME FROM OUTER SPACE: THE CHARLEVOIX METEOR CRATER AND BIOSPHERE RESERVE

THE METEOR

Every year tens of thousands of alien objects invade the earth's atmosphere. They are not, however, living beings guiding their spaceships to invade our planet; rather, they are massive space rocks known as meteors and range in size from a few centimetres to hundreds of metres across.

Few make it to the earth's surface, and those that do are called meteorites. In a few cases, they are large enough to explode and open up a crater in the earth's surface. The result is known as an impact crater. The largest impact crater in the world, the two-billion-year-old Vredefort crater at three hundred kilometres across, lies in a field in South Africa, but Canada can count more than two dozen impact craters of its own. None, however, has had the earth-altering impact of the fifteen-kilometre-wide asteroid that blasted into the shallow seas off Mexico's Yucatan Peninsula sixty-six million years ago, sending massive volumes of sulphur dust high into the atmosphere. The thick, poisonous cloud created a long, dark winter that wiped out the earth's food supply, starving the dinosaurs into a mass extinction.

Not all impact craters can be easily identified from the ground, including the one that plummeted into the Yucatan. Most require an aerial vantage or geological survey. Their evidence, however, is sometimes plain to see. A few even boast historical plaques to celebrate their locations.

Canada's largest meteor blew open the earth in today's Sudbury region of Ontario. When the massive object smashed into the earth 1.8 billion years ago, its fiery collision created a crater that originally measured 150 kilometres across and altered the region's chemistry enough to create an array of minerals, such as nickel and copper, that have made Sudbury the mining giant it is today. However, prolonged erosion and surface alteration has removed any visible crater formation, and only geological maps can reveal the shape and extent of the impact. Recent analyses have determined that the space intruder was, in fact, a comet and not the long-presumed asteroid.

One impact crater has become a major tourist attraction: the one near Flagstaff, Arizona, about two hours from the Grand Canyon. Exposed in a treeless desert, unobstructed by water or vegetation, it remains one of the world's most clearly identifiable craters and likely one of the most visited. That explosive collision occurred a mere fifty thousand years ago and blasted open a circular depression that is 1,300 metres wide and 130 metres deep. The visitor centre contains a fragment of the fiery rock.

A popular hiking trail in eastern Algonquin Park leads to the small 3.8-kilometre-wide Brent crater, largely filled in with small lakes. Even smaller is the Holleford crater, little more than a ninety-metre-wide depression in a farm field north of Kingston. Yet, both are the subject of nearby historical plaques.

And then there is the Charlevoix impact crater. At fifty-four kilometres across, it is the eleventh-largest crater on earth and has been described as the eighth wonder of the world. When the two-kilometre-wide monster meteorite roared into the earth 340 million years ago, it totally reconfigured the geology of the region, exploding upward with a force thousands of times that of the American atomic bomb that destroyed Hiroshima. The core of the upthrust is the visible Mont des Éboulements.

The southern half of the crater lies beneath the waters of the St. Lawrence River, while the northern portion is defined by the rugged Laurentian Mountains. The interior ring surrounding the upthrust is relatively level and remains home to a rural population, making it the earth's only inhabited impact crater. The outer ring consists of a higher ridge of largely Precambrian-era rocks.

The crater remained unknown until 1965, when Dr. Jehan Rondot studied a rock cut on the summit of Mont des Éboulements and saw the unusual shape of a shatter cone, literally a cone-shaped rock lined with clearly identifiable shatter lines.

The crater also has its own interpretation centre, the Observatoire de l'Astroblème, created by Professor Jean-Michel Gastonguay and located adjacent to the luxurious Fairmont Le Manoir Richelieu hotel at La Malbaie, Quebec. The building is actually the former golf clubhouse for the Manoir. Throughout the Charlevoix region, geological evidence of the huge explosion lies everywhere, from suevite beds (looking like grey lava flows) on the shores of the St. Lawrence River to fractures in limestone cliffs near La Malbaie.

From a distance, especially from the parking lot at the Observatoire, the level plain that surrounds the peak and the cone-shaped apex of the upthrust itself are all readily identifiable. Another fine view of the

A product of the Charlevoix meteor impact, this geological deformation known as a shatter cone is on display at the Astroblème de Charlevoix museum in Malbaie, Quebec.

On these mountains and cliffs in Hautes-Gorges-de-la-Rivière-Malbaie National Park, Charlevoix, Quebec, tundra vegetation can be seen — an extraordinary find in a place located so far south.

depression encircling the cone is that from Mont de la Croix at Saint-Hilarion.

Satellite imagery continues to reveal previously unknown craters in Canada, such as the twenty-five-kilometre-wide crater discovered on the Prince Albert Peninsula in the Arctic in 2012 and a buried crater in southern Alberta identified in 2014.

THE CHARLEVOIX UNESCO WORLD BIOSPHERE RESERVE

The best overview of the crater, however, is from a lookout high atop the Mont du Lac-des-Cygnes in the Parc national des Grands-Jardins north of Baie-Saint-Paul. The park also forms the core region of the Charlevoix UNESCO World Biosphere Reserve.

The Charlevoix Biosphere Reserve was originally established in 1988. (It briefly lost its status due to inaction but was reinstated in 2013.) The 457,000-hectare reserve contains 30,000 residents divided between the town of Baie-Saint-Paul and the rural zones around it.

Extending from the tidal flats of the St. Lawrence River to the rounded rocky summits of the Parc national des Grands-Jardins, the reserve is covered with forest zones that range from the hardwood maples of the lower reaches to the boreal forests in the Grands-Jardins and the tundra-covered summits of the mountains three hundred metres above the river. In particular, the Taiga Walk leads to the most southerly examples of Arctic vegetation in Canada.

Highway 381 leads north from Baie-Saint-Paul to the visitor centre for the park, where the map and guide to the tundra areas is available. Overall, the reserve covers 1,290,000 hectares, including part of the river, while the core encompasses 63,400 hectares.

While the biosphere's forests form the habitat for caribou, wolf, and cougar, the river is home to the beluga and blue whales.

Among those carrying out the biosphere's educational mandate is Centre Écologique du Port-au-Saumon, situated on the St. Lawrence River, which offers youth summer camps focused on the area's natural ecology.

The administrative focus of the World Biosphere Reserve lies with the Coop de l'arbre in Baie-Saint-Paul, in a structure that incorporates 70 percent recyclable material into its building materials and its operations. The Coop de l'arbre coordinates education with local schools and engages in eco-consulting with roughly a hundred area businesses.

A relaxing way to explore the region is to leave the car at the Hotel la Ferme in Baie-Saint-Paul and board the Charlevoix tourist train, which runs 125 kilometres along the scenic cliff-lined shores of the St. Lawrence River between Montmorency Falls east of Quebec City and La Malbaie.

THREE

HEADLESS VALLEY AND OTHER GRAND CANYONS

While Canada's many canyons may lack the layered splendours of Arizona's overcrowded Grand Canyon, the immensity of the remote Copper Canyon in Mexico, or the intimidating depth of the Colca Canyon in southern Peru (twice the depth of the Grand Canyon), the country is carved by many awe-inspiring gorges that draw the admiration of the world's hikers, photographers, rafters, canoers, and ordinary nature lovers.

Few are more inspirational than the remote, soaring walls of the South Nahanni River in Canada's Northwest Territories. Unique among river systems, the Nahanni existed before the mountains began to form. Early in its history, the river flowed across a vast plateau, but as the ground rose, the river's path cut ever deeper into the plateau, forming a deep, rocky gorge.

The river begins its five-hundred-kilometre dash in the Mackenzie Mountains before joining the Liard River near its junction with the great Mackenzie River. Foaming through daunting gorges, the river is a place of mysteries, headless corpses, and even stories of cannibalism. The names tell the story: the Funeral Range, the Headless Range, the Broken Skull River, and the Deadmen Valley.

From its source, the river flows serenely southeast through the Ragged Ranges. As the name suggests, these peaks are unlike mountains elsewhere. Soaring vertical rock towers like the Lotus Tower and the Cirque of the Unclimbables, a sheer granite wall that soars 2,740 metres above the valley, have been likened to the cliffs of El Capitane in the United States' Yosemite National Park. Here, too, the river flows past the Rabbitkettle hot springs, which bubble from the ground in a mound filled with multicoloured pools and ledges.

Then, at the spectacular Virginia Falls, the river loses that tranquility as it plunges through a series of channels, cascading through rocky gorges from a height twice that of Niagara Falls.

Here it begins its passage through some of North America's most dramatic canyons. Through the Third Canyon carved into the Funeral Range, it races beneath vertical cliffs that soar 1,600 metres above the river. The torrent then narrows to one hundred metres in width as it roars through The Gate, in which the Pulpit Rock defiantly stands as a rocky tower in the middle of the raging waters.

Next the river cuts through the Headless Mountains and opens into the Deadmen Valley, where gold seekers Willie and Frank McLeod mysteriously vanished in 1903, leaving only a note that read, "We have found a prospect." Their headless bodies were discovered in 1908, giving rise to yet another appropriately named gorge, the Valley of the Disappearing Men.

After surging through First Canyon, with its vertical canyon walls, the river comes to another set of hot springs that have created a microclimate that permits the growth of unusually lush vegetation, a phenomenon that gave rise to yet another Nahanni legend, namely that the area held a mysterious hidden tropical paradise.

In 1972 Canada's then prime minister, Pierre Trudeau, after canoeing the river, recommended it as a national park. In 1978 UNESCO designated it as its first World Heritage Site. In 1987 it became a Canadian Heritage River.

Many visitors will opt to go to Fort Simpson and fly in to view the incredible power of Virginia Falls as it plunges into a gorge deeper than that at Niagara Falls. For those hiking or rafting, the park offers four campgrounds and more than a dozen hiking trails, most of them multi-day trips. Rafting adventures begin above Virginia Falls and may continue for up to eight days before reaching the Liard River. The park headquarters is in Fort Simpson, Northwest Territories.

While it may be the nation's most spectacular canyon, the Nahanni is not Canada's only stunning, or even unusual, gorge. The Maligne River in Jasper National Park starts off as a normal-looking river winding through the mountains, until it suddenly disappears into the limestone formation, a phenomenon known as karst geology. After it re-emerges, it plunges into a canyon fifty metres deep but a mere two metres wide.

Myra Canyon is a bowl-shaped canyon rising more than 915 metres above the Okanagan Valley in southern British Columbia. It has become famous not so much for its stunning beauty but rather for its railway trestles. In 1915 the chief engineer for the Kettle Valley Railway, Andrew McCulloch, needed a way to run his tracks along the top of the canyon. He cut the rail bed into the rock walls and crossed the deep gullies with a string of eighteen trestles.

From the rail bed, those walls plunged steeply to the valley below. While this didn't faze the railway crews, following the line's abandonment the rail bed was converted into a rail trail, providing some of the most dizzying trestle crossings in the cycling world and making it one of North America's most sought-after cycling experiences. Devastating forest fires in 2003 and again in 2013 burned most of the trestles, but they were rebuilt and continue to lure and awe the world's cyclists.

In the 1910s, the Group of Seven discovered the stunning beauty of Algoma's mountains and would often venture deep into the Agawa Canyon in Ontario. There they would sketch the rugged beauty that appears in their now-famous works. The canyon dates back 1.2 billion years, when erosion and glaciers scraped out a fault line in the rock to create the canyon. Today, visitors can use the beautiful hiking trails or enjoy a train tour that departs from Sault Ste. Marie.

Known as Ontario's Grand Canyon, the Ouimet Canyon suddenly appears to the traveller who follows the trail from the parking area to the rim of a high plateau overlooking the Lake Superior lowlands. Although only one hundred and fifty metres wide, the canyon plunges between sheer cliffs to a valley floor more than thirty metres below and extends several kilometres through the plateau. During the many ice ages that blanketed Ontario, the mighty ice tongues ground into and eroded a diabase sill, a softer rock that allowed the ice to create the gorge while the harder walls remained in place.

The columnar rock walls have eroded to create unusual sights, such as a free-standing pillar known as the Indians Head. The bottom of the canyon lies in darkness for much of the day, enabling snow to linger into June and vegetation more common to the Arctic to grow there. Situated in a provincial park

Hiking trails in the beautiful Agawa Canyon, located in the Agawa Canyon Wilderness Park, Algoma District, Ontario, are accessible from the popular Agawa Canyon Tour Train.

a short distance from the Trans-Canada Highway, the site is free of the commercialization that often surrounds other prominent natural features.

A short distance east of the Ouimet Canyon, a similar defile, the Eagle Canyon, offers a more daunting experience. Here, a company called Eagle Canyon Adventures has constructed Canada's longest suspension foot bridge, extending more than two hundred metres across the gorge and fifty metres above it. In addition, there is a (slightly) less intimidating bridge a short distance away that stretches a hundred metres across the gorge and stands forty metres above the valley floor.

Now a famous tourist attraction in British Columbia, the older Capilano Suspension Bridge is strung across the Capilano River canyon. Originally

Horseshoe Canyon is located in the world-famous Drumheller Badlands in central Alberta.

built in 1889, the bridge extends 137 metres across the valley floor, which lies more than 70 metres below. The canyon today also includes a cantilevered walkway that clings to the granite cliffs as well as a canopy walk through the trees. The site has been described as Vancouver's top tourist attraction.

Another of Ontario's more stunning gorges lies in a remote corner of the popular Algonquin Provincial Park. Known as the Barron Canyon, it formed near the close of the last ice age more than ten thousand years ago when an ice dam that held back the glacier's rising meltwaters collapsed suddenly, releasing a torrent estimated as having the force of a thousand Niagaras.

As the waters raced eastward, they gouged out a softer fault line in the hard rocks and created

One of the many spectacular waterfalls to be found in the majestic Nahanni National Park Reserve is the Victoria Falls in the Dehcho Region of the Northwest Territories.

the hundred-metre-deep gorge. While the Barron River once echoed with the yells of loggers floating their timber downstream, today it is the domain of canoeists. The rim of the canyon lies unfenced at the end of a 1.5-kilometre trail.

Located forty-one kilometres northeast of Quebec City, Canyon Sainte-Anne is one of that province's more unusual gorges. The sixty-metre-deep canyon has three suspension bridges that allow the hundred thousand annual visitors to view the unusual geological "potholes" and the torrent of the foaming Sainte-Anne waterfalls. The site remained inaccessible until a road was built in 1973.

Alberta's stunning Drumheller Badlands offer not just dinosaur bones but also a pair of similarly named spectacular canyons: Horsethief and Horseshoe Canyons. Horsethief Canyon, accessible by trail from Highway 838, derives its name from legends of horse thieves rebranding stolen horses and even plotting a smuggling route. Horseshoe Canyon, close to Highway 9, earns its name from its bowl-like shape. It, too, is part of the badlands formation and offers views from the rim over this unusual geological formation.

Both canyons, as well as the badlands, owe their origins to the raging glacial meltwaters that eroded into the sandstones of the region more than ten thousand years ago. After travelling through the rolling wheat fields and ranchland, coming suddenly upon the badlands' deep gullies and oddly shaped rock columns known as hoodoos is something of a visual shock. It is a landscape that the *Globe and Mail* has described as "found in only a few places on earth." Part of the badlands formation, the nearby Dinosaur Provincial Park has yielded a treasure trove of dinosaur bones, many of which are now displayed at the Royal Tyrrell Museum near Drumheller.

On a distant island at the mouth of the St. Lawrence River estuary, Anticosti Island National Park contains one of Canada's lesser-known waterfalls and canyons. Vaureal Falls plunges 76 metres into the Vaureal River and then along a canyon 90 metres deep, 3.2 kilometres long, and 9 kilometres from the river's outlet into the Gulf of St. Lawrence. The falls is accessible by car 150 kilometres from the island's sole community, Port-Menier. Although comparable in size to Prince Edward Island, the island claims only two hundred residents, but is also home to a population of 150,000 rather friendly white-tailed deer. In 2017 there was a local move to encourage the federal government to submit the island to UNESCO for designation as a World Heritage Site. The only access to the island itself is by ferry from Sept-Îles or by air.

FOUR

THE GIANT'S RIB:
THE NIAGARA ESCARPMENT WORLD BIOSPHERE RESERVE

It is Canada's longest linear biosphere reserve. It contains rare flora and unusual rock formations and is a great place for hiking, caving, and scenic driving. At 725 kilometres long and 1,923 square kilometres in area, it is Ontario's distinctive Niagara Escarpment. Due to its shape and configuration, it has been nicknamed the Giant's Rib.

Its roots date back 450 million years; the North American continent of that time bore no resemblance to that of today. At that time, a basin where Michigan sits today was filling with water to form an inland sea. Sand, silt, and coral settled to the bottom and began to harden. At 350 million years ago, the seas dried up, leaving the sediments exposed and tilting like a shallow bowl upward to the adjacent mountains to the east, whose roots today form the Canadian Shield.

Wind and water began to wear away the fringes. The softer lower shales eroded fairly easily, while the harder surface dolostones and limestone formed a protective cap rock. This differential erosion gave the escarpment the cliff-face profile that it has today.

The erosion continued as a series of ice ages that lasted over a million years — the latest of which peaked between eighteen thousand and twenty thousand years ago — wore the rocks away even more, carving a string of wide re-entrant valleys while freeze-thaw cycles caused great chunks of limestone to break away, forming a number of fissure caves.

The mighty limestone ridge actually rises at Rochester, New York, crosses the Niagara River into Ontario at Queenston, and runs straight to Hamilton, where it is locally known as Hamilton Mountain. Here, it is interrupted by the Dundas Valley before running north from Hamilton toward Georgian Bay.

Along the way, many geological features stand out. Cliff faces and mesa-like promontories at Mount Nemo and Rattlesnake Point and several scenic valleys are among the most vivid.

The most dramatic gorge of the ridge is that which was carved out to form the Forks of the Credit Canyon. Here, amid soaring cliffs, the two branches of the Credit River tumble together.

Near the village of Cheltenham, south of Orangeville, erosion has exposed a feature known as Ontario's Badlands. Here, early pioneer clearing exposed the underlying Medina shale, with its alternating layers of hard red and greenish clay. With vegetation unable

The Cheltenham Badlands, part of the Niagara Escarpment, are distinguished by their red and greenish layers, the result of alternating high and low concentrations of iron oxide in the shale.

to regain a foothold, the elements have eroded the exposed slopes into a series of colourful gullies, reminiscent of the Alberta Badlands or New Mexico's Painted Desert. So distinctive and striking is this formation that it has attracted increasing numbers of day-trippers as well as moviemakers seeking unusual settings.

At Orangeville, the ridge no longer remains visible, for it is here that Ontario's other great geographical feature, the Oak Ridges Moraine, a massive glacial deposit, covers the escarpment's face completely.

North of Orangeville, the escarpment re-emerges, displaying scenic re-entrant valleys that carry the Mad, Noisy, and Pine Rivers. The ridge reaches its highest and most scenic point at Georgian Peaks, where it rises three hundred metres above the waters of Georgian Bay. From here it bends westward, hugging the shore of the bay, to the Beaver Valley, the escarpment's longest valley. Two other re-entrant valleys, now beneath the water of the bay, form the sheltered harbours at Owen Sound and Wiarton.

From that point, the ridge extends northward and forms the eastern coastline of the Bruce Peninsula, with stunning rock formations and dark caves. The ridge then slips under the water of Georgian Bay at the one-time fishing port of Tobermory before re-emerging to form the backbone of Manitoulin Island.

When the glaciers of the last ice age finally receded back north, rivers and creeks began to cut into the cliffs, further deepening the gorges and creating the waterfalls that line the escarpment today.

The largest and most celebrated of these is Niagara Falls, often labelled as a world wonder. This mighty cataract started when the waters of an earlier Lake Erie, freed from the glaciers' ice dams, began flowing northward, plunging over the cliffs where Queenston sits today. For ten thousand years, the relentless forces of ice and water eroded the river back to where it is today to form the thundering Niagara Falls. Geologists believe that this erosion will continue until the brink reaches Lake Erie in another ten thousand years; the falls will then be reduced to little more than a set of rapids.

Throughout the length of the formation, hundreds of other waterfalls tumble over the cliffs and into the gorges. No exact count exists, although more than a hundred have been counted in the Hamilton region alone. Documenting waterfalls has become a pastime in itself. Criteria have been developed to define "waterfall," namely, the fall must drop a minimum of three metres, be at least one metre wide, and contain a flow of water for at least part of each year.

In the seventeenth century, European explorers like Samuel de Champlain arrived. In 1680, Father Louis Hennepin was the first European explorer to lay eyes on the mighty torrent of the falls.

Beginning in 1784 Loyalist refugees fleeing from the American Revolution were given lands in the area, forcing many First Nations Peoples to relocate.

The escarpment also played a key role in the War of 1812, when the Americans tried unsuccessfully to take over Canada. The British troops, under Major General Isaac Brock, and First Nations warriors, successfully repelled an American attack on Queenston Heights, but Brock was killed shortly after the fighting began. A monument at Queenston Heights (the third to be built there) salutes his gallantry.

In June 1813 the Battle of Stoney Creek raged beneath the heights when a surprise nighttime raid by the British once again sent the Americans scurrying for home. This victory, too, is celebrated at the Battlefield House and monument at Stoney Creek, along with annual re-enactments.

Also in June 1813, the most legendary feat of the war occurred when Laura Secord, living in Queenston, overheard American troops who were billeted at her father's house planning an attack against British commander Lieutenant FitzGibbon, whose headquarters stood atop the cliffs nearby. Helped by First Nations warriors, Secord was able to make her way undetected through the woods and up the cliff to alert FitzGibbon, whose troops and warriors turned back the attack. While only the foundations of the FitzGibbon house remain today, the more modest Secord house has been preserved in Queenston and is a National Historic Site.

The success in turning back the Americans opened the way for more settlers to flock into the area. Rivers and creeks began to sprout mills, and rough trails wound through the woods, opening lands for farming.

In the 1820s the success of Erie Canal in New York State prompted William Hamilton Merritt to propose an all-Canadian canal from Port Dalhousie on Lake Ontario to Lake Erie. However, the Niagara Escarpment, with its steep rock face, stood in the way. Merritt won the financial and political support that he needed, and in 1828 the Welland Canal opened to schooners and barges as far away as Port Robinson and eventually to Port Colborne on Lake Erie. But it took forty-two wooden locks to get the boats there, half of them to mount the escarpment alone.

In the 1840s and 1870s the canal was widened and deepened, the number of locks reduced to twenty-seven, and the wooden locks replaced with ones of stone. In 1932 the Lake Ontario entrance was moved to Port Weller and the number of locks reduced to eight. The climb up the cliff was achieved with a set of three twin flight locks where the water flowed directly from one lock into the next. These were paired to allow ships to lock through in both directions concurrently.

Today the passage of the now mighty ships takes a mere eight hours rather than eight days. A popular visitor centre at Lock Station 3 in St. Catharines contains a museum and an elevated viewing platform overlooking the lock, where visitors can see close up the mighty vessels inch through the tight quarters.

In 1853 the railway age arrived with the completion of the Great Western Railway from Niagara Falls to Sarnia. Industry fled their water-powered mill sites and moved trackside.

While bypassing the early mill sites, the railways brought prosperity to Niagara Escarpment cities like Niagara Falls and Hamilton and towns in between.

By the 1850s and 1860s the farmlands of southern Ontario were quickly filling. Mill villages thrived along the escarpment's rivers and creeks. The railway reached the ports of Collingwood, Thornbury, Meaford, Owen Sound, and Wiarton in the 1870s, and industry followed suit.

While lumbering drove the economy of the Bruce Peninsula, most of its soils were poor, and once the forests were depleted, the region, lacking railways, stagnated.

During this period, except for the booming popularity of Niagara Falls and its daredevils, the recreational potential of the escarpment escaped notice. Then, following the Second World War, the cities began to grow and urbanites became more mobile, seeking out recreation opportunities in the surrounding countryside and along the scenic Niagara Escarpment in particular.

As that same growth sprawled ever outward, the potential of the escarpment became compromised. In particular, pits and quarries carved unsightly gaps in the limestone rock and threatened the groundwater, while large rural estates gobbled up extensive tracts of field and forest.

To encourage the recreational appreciation of the Niagara Escarpment, in 1960 a group of naturalists embarked on the task of creating a trail along the ridge, comparable to the popular Appalachian Trail in the eastern United States. The job involved visiting private landowners along the proposed route to gain their permission to use their lands for the trail. Most agreed, and in 1967 cairns were unveiled, one in Queenston and one in Tobermory, to mark the southern and northern termini of the trail. The Bruce Trail was born.

Every year, thousands of hikers are drawn to the Bruce Trail, but are especially challenged in the Bruce Peninsula portion, where the rocky clifftops rise above the tossing waters of Georgian Bay. Still, the trail remains a work in progress, its location on private lands dependent on the goodwill of the landowners. As ownership changes hands, some reject the use of the trail, while others invite it.

In 1968 a new school of planning thought was emerging at the University of Waterloo, namely regional planning and government. Dr. Ralph Krueger, head of the school's Geography and Planning Department, could see that unfettered sprawl was overwhelming the fruit lands of the Niagara Peninsula, so he proposed a form of regional government to bring it under control.

Such planning was critical in this region, for it is here along the Niagara Peninsula that the escarpment wall helps retain the moderating influence of Lake Ontario, allowing for a lengthened growing season that permits the growing of a range of tender fruits, such as peaches, plums, and cherries, a microclimate found nowhere else in Ontario.

In 1968 Professor Len Gertler, in the same Geography and Planning Department, authored a comprehensive report identifying the many land-use threats to the entire escarpment and proposed

planning controls with a series of parks linked by trails, helping the Bruce Trail to secure a more permanent route.

In light of the report, the Ontario government created the Niagara Escarpment Planning Commission, tasked to come up with control mechanisms to preserve the features of the ridge. Public consultations became acrimonious, as many landowners and small municipalities objected to controls over their lands.

Acceptance of the plan was helped when, in 1990, UNESCO inscribed the entire escarpment area as a UNESCO World Biosphere Reserve, although the designation itself offers no regulatory controls over use or development. Finally, in 1994 the province approved a plan that featured different levels of control, ranging from acquisition to limited growth to compatible growth, policies to which local zoning must conform.

While the integrity of the ridge is today overseen by many methods, protecting the features can prove a challenge. The unusual exposed badlands at Cheltenham became so popular that overuse prompted the closure of the feature in 2015 while more protective measures were put in place.

New provincial parks were established and conservation areas were added, including at Short Hills near Fonthill, Forks of the Credit near Orangeville, and Mono Cliffs, while a new national park was created on the Bruce Peninsula and a marine park established to protect the waters and the shipwrecks around its tip.

Of the many new parks, Forks of the Credit Provincial Park reveals the Niagara Escarpment's most

Flowerpot Island, near Tobermory, Ontario, is an unusual result of the ongoing erosion of the cliffs of the Niagara Escarpment.

stunning scenery. The park follows the canyon of the Credit River, where steep cliffs rise on each side. Ruins of the Deagle gristmill and power plant rest beside a plunging waterfall. The canyon then merges with another branch of the river to form the forks.

That branch leads to the small but attractive Belfountain Conservation Area, where the stone landscaping of an early owner remains beside another steep waterfall.

The northern tip of the peninsula has become the Bruce Peninsula National Park, with campgrounds, trails, and rare rock formations, such as the Grotto cave and the strange flowerpot rock formations, the limestone "chimneys" on Flowerpot Island. Due to the incredible number of ships wrecked while trying to round the dangerous tip of the peninsula, the waters have become the Fathom Five Marine National Park, increasingly popular with divers. Some of the wrecks are even visible from the surface.

Ontario's most popular ski hills are found on the high slopes of Blue Mountain and Georgian Peaks, which also offer wide views of Georgian Bay far below, views that are easily seen in the summer as well.

Amid its many parks, the escarpment offers up a few secrets. One of these is Silent Valley. This wooded oasis lies well off the beaten path and is accessed by a dead-end concession road east of Owen Sound as well as a side trail from the Bruce Trail.

While not yet a park, the trails through Silent Valley begin with a plaque that describes the features along its paths. These include rare rock formations and the hidden, overgrown remains of an early farmstead, where the deep stone-lined well remains visible.

Beyond the remains of the barn and rusting farm equipment lies one of the escarpment's most unusual sights, the wreckage of a small aircraft. In 1970 the four-seater was approaching Griffith Island just off Owen Sound when a violent storm tore the plane apart in midair, sending it plummeting to the ground. None of the four passengers survived. The wreckage wasn't found until 2014, and it remains there to this day. The Bruce Trail Foundation now owns the property.

Along the 725-kilometre ridge lies a remarkable variety of forest regions. In the southern reaches, the Carolinian forest displays trees more typical of those found in the southern American states, such as the dogwood and tulip tree as well as the sassafras, while southern wildlife, such as the opossum, may be found as well.

The middle segment of the ridge finds mixed forests of conifer and deciduous tree species, while the hardier pines are more common to the north. One of the oldest of the Niagara Escarpment's trees is the slow-growing diminutive eastern white cedar, examples of which have been dated back a thousand years.

Much of the native wildlife has been wiped out, including the once-common timber rattlesnake, although bears, wolves, foxes, coyotes, and deer remain fairly common. Although in danger of extinction, the massasauga rattlesnake still lurks in the rocks and wetlands of the escarpment's more northern reaches.

Indeed, the escarpment offers as much history as it does beauty. The many waterfalls that tumble from the rim offered water power for mill operations and the villages that grew around them. Although the arrival of the railways and the clearing of the forests closed most such operations, their legacy can still be found in a number of locations.

The mill at the ghost town of Ball's Falls, dating from 1812, has become a museum, as has that at Morningstar Mill nearby. The stone walls of the gristmill in the Crooks Hollow Conservation Area recall its early days as a milling centre. The Ancaster Mill is now a popular restaurant, while the mill complex at Glen Williams on the Credit River near Georgetown has morphed into an artists' colony.

One of the Niagara Escarpment's resources was the underlying Medina shale used in brick making. Near the scenic village of Cheltenham, the massive ruins of the former Cheltenham brickworks dominate the roadside.

Situated on the Mad River, the pretty little town of Creemore contains a popular brewery and one of North America's smallest jails, a stone structure with just three cells.

The Noisy River once powered the mills at Dunedin, which, with its various empty structures, including a stone blacksmith shop, has become a virtual ghost town. A short distance farther north, in the hamlet of Glen Huron, tucked into the valley of the Mad River, the Hamilton Brothers mill still works away, using the power of the water in the river as it has since 1874.

To the west of Blue Mountain, Beaver Valley contains the ruins of a hydroelectric water power proposal that was abandoned before it began. The unusual stone arches of the abandoned tunnel system lie near the rim of Eugenia Falls in the Eugenia Falls Conservation Area. Here, too, a fake gold rush led to the surveying of a speculative town plan named Eugenia, which never grew. Inglis Falls, in Owen Sound, with the remains of its early mill operation, is a popular picnicking and hiking destination.

These do not represent the Niagara Escarpment's only legacy of ruins. The stunning scenery prompted many a millionaire to build their castles here, some of which now lie in ruin. High atop Spirit Rock, overlooking Wiarton, are the stone walls of the Corran, an 1881 mansion built by Alexander McNeill. It is situated in the Spirit Rock Conservation Area. Near Blue Mountain, the remote remains of Osler Castle are the sole legacy of the castle built in 1893 by wealthy Toronto lawyer Britton Bath Osler. He intended it as a bucolic retreat for his asthmatic wife, who, sadly, died soon after he finished it. Down in the Dundas Valley, the stone walls of the Hermitage are all that remain of a castle built in 1830 by Reverend George Sheed.

The protection of these many features has given rise to a new type of growth, the day-tripping market. Mills became museums, general stores were converted to antique shops, and restaurants opened in many of the scenic villages and hamlets. In the hamlet of Violet Hill, a popular restaurant called Mrs. Miller's occupies the former schoolhouse named after the school's last teacher. Heathcote and Kimberley in the Beaver Valley attract antique and wine enthusiasts as well as winter skiers, who use the escarpment's steep slopes.

Niagara Falls has morphed from the tackiness of the amusements on Clifton Hill to become a major casino hub. The fruit lands of the Niagara Peninsula, most of which are now protected through zoning, have attracted pick-your-own enthusiasts, while vineyards began to cover the slopes, creating an award-winning and growing wine industry. The apple bounty of the Beaver Valley draws visitors in the fall, especially to local businesses like Grandma Lambe's, renowned for its popular pies.

The many natural phenomena of the ridge lure more adventurous travellers as well. The mesas of Mount Nemo and Rattlesnake Point are among the more prominent features of the great cliff face. In fact, Rattlesnake Point is home to major rock-climbing schools. Collapsing rocks have created a number of fissure caves along the scarp face, popular with hikers and spelunkers alike. Besides the many fissure caves that fracture the face of the cliffs, more substantial cave systems occur at Scenic Caves near Collingwood and at Greig's Caves north of Wiarton, the latter being where scenes from the acclaimed stone-age movie *Quest for Fire* were filmed. Bruce's Caves east of Wiarton has also been a popular film location.

The unusual Crawford Lake in the Crawford Lake Conservation Area is one of only two meromictic lakes in Ontario, where the waters are so deep that the bottom deposits rest undisturbed by any currents or wave action. In those deposits, scientists discovered evidence of an early Indigenous settlement. Further investigation nearby located the site of an early longhouse and palisade, now reconstructed within the park.

Along the famed Bruce Peninsula, the cliffs plunge directly into Georgian Bay's waters, leaving unusual rock formations, such as the lion's head at the town of Lion's Head, the Grotto, and the unusual Flowerpot Island columnar limestone chimneys that have given rise to popular tour boat excursions from Tobermory.

Despite traffic congestion, the escarpment does contain several scenic roads. Ridge Road follows the rim of the escarpment from Stoney Creek to Grimsby, and the road to Cabot Head on the Bruce Peninsula hugs the shoreline while the cliffs loom above as it leads to the quiet one-time fishing village of Wingfield Basin, where the old wooden lighthouse now houses a museum. County Road 1 along the Georgian Bluffs offers scenic views between Wiarton and Owen Sound.

Between Rattlesnake Point and Georgian Bay, scenic roads dive in and out of the many wide valleys, where wide vistas extend from the valley walls.

The lookout from the top of Blue Mountain offers one of the province's most stunning vantages, with views extending across farmland and over the waters of Georgian Bay.

Happily, the Niagara Escarpment Commission's regulatory control, the 105 parks — including three provincial parks and two national parks, Bruce Peninsula National Park and Fathom Five Marine National Park — as well as conservation areas, nature reserves, the Bruce Trail Conservancy, and municipal parks, all combine to ensure that this great feature will endure as one of Canada's world wonders.

FIVE

ROCKY MOUNTAINS HIGH

To the traveller motoring across the flatlands of Canada's Prairie provinces, there suddenly appears on the horizon a seemingly impenetrable white-topped grey wall. As the traveller approaches, the wall takes on a craggy sawtooth profile but is still seemingly impenetrable. These are the iconic and world-famous Canadian Rocky Mountains.

Born of a relentless slow-motion collision of two tectonic plates, the mountains stretch more than 1,200 kilometres from Alaska to Montana, but their fame lies within Canada.

Many millions of years ago, the earth's continents were but a single land mass. When the mass began to split, the sections that were to become North and South America began to creep westward at the rate of a centimetre each century. After more millions of years went by, the west-moving plate encountered a smaller plate that was moving eastward.

As the east-moving plate plunged beneath the west-moving one, the leading edge was thrust upward into a series of rocky ridges. The easternmost ridge became the Rockies. Today that crumpled chain claims fifty peaks that rise more than 3,350 metres above sea level, Mount Robson being the highest at nearly 4,000 metres.

Geologists have differentiated individual mountains by their shape and formation. Those whose layers and towers resemble European castles are called castellated, such as the aptly named Castle Mountain west of Banff. Mount Rundle displays a classic uplifted layer, with one side sloping up to a jagged peak and a sharp drop down the other side displaying its ancient layers of rock. Mount Assiniboine is a perfect example of a Matterhorn, where four sides have been sculpted by glacial action, leaving a small, flat top. Then there are anticlinal mountains, where the layers are pushed up into a dome, as in Moose Mountain, and synclinal mountains, where the layers are pushed together downward to form a depression, as in Mount Kerkeslin near Jasper.

Despite their daunting barrier to the easterner, the mountains' secret passageways were well known to their earliest inhabitants, the Ktunaxa Kinbasket. Early European explorers learned of these routes, including Alexander Mackenzie, who came through the Peace River country, followed by Simon Fraser in 1895, while David Thompson spent the years 1799 to 1803 mapping and surveying the region. Their quest: finding furs.

Located approximately halfway between Banff and Lake Louise in Banff National Park, Castle Mountain was named by James Hector in 1858 for its castle-like appearance.

Several decades later, more surveyors arrived — those for the railways. Seeking a route for Canada's grand national dream, the Canadian Pacific Railway, the surveyors identified three possible ways through the Rockies. The Yellowhead Pass was considered too far north, the Crowsnest Pass was thought to be too far south, but the Kicking Horse Pass, roughly in the middle, seemed just right.

The railway builders, however, saw more than just a way to the west. The CPR's inveterate general manager, one William Cornelius Van Horne, recognized that money was to be made from wealthy tourists and claimed, "If we can't export the scenery, we'll import the tourists." It helped considerably when three of his employees discovered hot springs near what is today's Banff, and Van Horne decided that this would be the ideal spot to lure his tourists.

Near this site, he began construction of a grand hotel, now the stunning chateauesque Fairmont Banff Springs, and convinced his friends in government to protect the area by creating Canada's first national park in 1885: Banff National Park.

It didn't take long for Banff to become a focus for artists, many of whom were hired by the railway itself. These included John Fraser and Frederic M. Bell-Smith. The Banff School of Fine Arts opened its doors in 1935 and welcomed such Group of Seven luminaries as Arthur Lismer, Lawren Harris, and JEH MacDonald. The town continues to be an internationally renowned focus for the arts, including the Banff Centre for Arts and Creativity and the annual Banff Summer Arts Festival.

Using postcards and posters, the CPR turned the Rocky Mountains into a world-famous destination. Adjacent to the new park, other national parks quickly followed: Glacier National Park in 1886, Yoho National Park in 1886, and Waterton Lakes National Park in 1895.

More hotels inevitably followed as well, including the Chateau Lake Louise and the Prince of Wales Hotel in the Waterton Lakes National Park. While many of the railway dining halls that the CPR built along its line bloomed into hotels as well, in subsequent years these succumbed to railway modernization and, of course, the auto age. None survive.

Overlooked by the focus on the southern parks, Jasper National Park was created in 1907. It has become the focus of the Jasper Park Lodge and is the jumping-off point for VIA Rail's Skeena train through the mountains to Prince Rupert, a scenic two-day rail journey that overnights in Prince George.

The opening of the Trans-Canada Highway through the Rockies in 1966 meant that more and more tourists were arriving by car, and those preferring the train dwindled. In a last-ditch effort to lure travellers back to the tracks, in 1966 the CPR introduced its stunning new chrome streamliner train set, the Canadian. That route was soon discontinued by the short-sighted Mulroney government in 1990. Today it is the world-acclaimed Rocky Mountaineer that has inherited the CPR's historic route, adding several additional scenic mountain experiences throughout British Columbia.

However, most of the millions of yearly visitors arrive by automobile or on the thousands of tour coaches that stream in, carrying the curious from all parts of the globe. Within the Rocky Mountains Parks are many National Historic Sites. Banff National Park alone contains a thousand glaciers, a ghost town, and the country's highest town at 1,384 metres above sea level.

In Banff, the Cave and Basin National Historic Site represents the site of the first hot springs discovery, which was the impetus to start tourism to the Rockies. In Glacier National Park, the Rogers Pass National Historic Site marks the last elusive passage that challenged the CPR's surveyors.

The Banff Park Museum is in one of the area's oldest buildings, a 1903 log pagoda-style building.

Parks Canada describes it, with its two-storey cross-log construction, as "the largest and most elaborate example of the early phase of the rustic design tradition in the national parks of Canada." Nearby, the Abbot Pass Refuge is a stone shelter built in 1922 by Swiss guides hired by the CPR to bring more skiers to the park. The Skoki Lodge was added in 1931, built by a ski group, and remains accessible only to skiers or hikers.

Also known as Highway 93, the spectacular Icefields Parkway has been described by the National Geographic Society as one of the world's "must-see" scenic drives. It extends for 280 stunning kilometres from the Trans-Canada Highway 1 at Lake Louise to Trans-Canada Highway 16 near Jasper and follows a trench that defines the west side of the Rockies.

Along this route, the spectacular scenery never seems to end and includes the blue-green waters of Bow Lake (so coloured due to the lake's glacial origins), with Crowfoot Glacier clinging to the mountainside on the opposite shore. The highway then twists up out of the valley to a hairpin bend, where a lookout reveals the mountain-lined valley extending far below.

The high point for most, however, is a walk on a glacier. At the Glacier Discovery Centre, tourists are invited to board a SnoCoach to travel up the Athabasca Glacier, a tongue of ice extending from the Columbia Icefield that covers the mountains beyond.

Continuing north from the Discovery Centre (which offers meals, accommodation, washrooms, and a depiction of the story of the rapidly retreating glacier), the traveller will encounter one of the route's newer features, the Glacier Skywalk, a semicircular

A glacier-fed lake, Peyto Lake is only one of the stunning features found along the Icefields Parkway in Banff National Park.

glass-bottomed platform that extends dizzyingly out over the 280-metre-deep valley (not unlike that which challenges the timid at the Grand Canyon). Before the parkway ends at Highway 16, it also gives access to the foaming cataract at Athabasca Falls.

Farther south, lying on the U.S. border, Waterton Lakes National Park is 505 square kilometres in area and home to the deepest lake in the Rockies. The Prince of Wales Hotel, built in 1927 by the American Great Northern Railway, offers stunning views of

Waterton Lake through its large plate-glass windows reinforced against the fierce winds that race through the mountain passes and along the lake.

The park includes such scenic drives as the Red Rock Parkway, a bison paddock where the shaggy beasts are free to roam in their natural grassland habitat, and the site of Alberta's first oil well at Oil City.

It would be no surprise, then, when in 1988 UNESCO inscribed the Canadian Rocky Mountain Parks as a World Heritage Site, noting that they "exemplify outstanding physical features, including remnant valley glaciers, canyons, and possess excellent natural beauty."

This was not UNESCO's first designation in the Rockies. Years earlier, in 1980, the agency had identified the Burgess Shale as "one of the most significant fossil areas in the world." The fossil sites were later enfolded into the larger heritage site.

SIX

JURASSIC PARK NORTH: ALBERTA'S WORLD-FAMOUS DINOSAUR GRAVEYARDS

THE DINOSAUR BEDS

Southern Alberta is world famous for its vast area of buried dinosaur fossils, many of them intact. So much so that in 1979 the area known as Dinosaur Provincial Park was designated as a UNESCO World Heritage Site.

More than three hundred different dinosaur specimens and an incredible 150 complete skeletons have been unearthed in the exposed sediments of these spectacular badlands, including every known species of Cretaceous dinosaur.

The age of the dinosaurs dates back to between 231 million years ago and 96 million years ago. During the Cretaceous period, the area was similar to today's Florida, flat and subtropical, and it was home to thirty-five species of dinosaur, including birds, reptiles, amphibians, and even early mammals. As they died, they fell into layers of mud and were gradually covered by layers of sand and clay. Over millions of years, the sediments built up.

As the last ice age receded, the meltwaters poured over the region, creating deep gullies in the dry conditions. And there, exposed in the eroded hills, appeared the skeletal remains of one of the world's most extensive dinosaur graveyards.

Throughout the late 1800s, as the scientific community began to take increasing interest in the study of dinosaurs, paleontologists began to explore the exposed layers, particularly along a twenty-seven-kilometre stretch of the Red Deer River in southern Alberta. Although many of the specimens unearthed here are now in museums around the world, the greatest number are on display in the Royal Tyrrell Museum of Palaeontology in Drumheller, Alberta.

Dinosaur Provincial Park offers a variety of nature trails, including one to the 1913 quarry where many of the dinosaur bones were originally found. Tours begin at the visitor centre, which contains an eighty-seat theatre and interactive exhibits.

The focus for the dinosaur displays themselves lies with the Royal Tyrrell Museum of Palaeontology in Drumheller. Opened in 1985, it contains the world's most extensive display of full fossils. Here, a twenty-five-minute video introduces the many scientists whose passion and commitment have led to expanding the world's knowledge of the finds. Another video reveals the secrets of fossil preservation.

Of the fossils on display, one of the most unusual is the rare *Dimetrodon*, a mammal-like dinosaur that represents the evolution of the earth's mammals more than 250 million years ago. "Cretaceous Alberta" depicts four examples of the mighty *Albertosaurus* creature depicted in its natural habitat.

All visitors, young and old, inevitably make their way into the Dinosaur Hall, where they come face to bone with the Hollywood favourite, *T. rex*, star of the Jurassic Park films. Here, too, is the three-horned *Triceratops* as well as the familiar long-necked *Stegosaurus* and the giant *Camarasaurus*. The largest of the creatures is the twenty-one-metre crocodile-like seaborne *Ichthyosaur* unearthed in northern British Columbia from the shores of the Sikanni Chief River.

In March 2011 an excavator operator working at Suncor's Millennium Mine in northern Alberta struck something he hadn't expected. What he was seeing were not bones but rather a nearly perfectly intact dinosaur itself, skin and all. Palaeontologists from the Tyrrell Museum raced north in a private Suncor jet. There they were astonished to see something they had not realized even existed, a new subspecies of *Nodosaur*. Its preservation was closer to mummification than fossilization.

Protected by a skin of thorny armour, this vegetarian measured more than five metres long and lived around 110 to 120 million years ago. Its fate likely came when it died and was covered in water and clay, helping to preserve the carcass. Indeed, its preservation is so complete that even its skin colouration can be discerned. But the protective armour has also prevented scientists from probing its skeletal structure.

In May 2017 the Royal Tyrrell Museum put the remarkable new find on display as part of its "industrial discovery" theme. The revelation made news worldwide and was featured in *National Geographic* magazine and on CNN.

Opened in 1985, the museum bears the name of Joseph Burr Tyrrell, who came across the first of the finds while surveying coal seams in the Red Deer Valley. Today the 4,400-square-metre facility contains more than 130,000 examples of plants, insects, and, of course, the mighty beasts themselves from the age of the dinosaurs. The museum offers field trips and hands-on lessons on preserving the ancient specimens.

Capitalizing on its dinosaur fame, the town of Drumheller has created the "world's largest dinosaur," a *T. rex* that stands twenty-five metres high (four times that of a real *T. rex*) and contains stairs to the gaping, tooth-filled mouth. The town now bills itself as the dinosaur capital of the world. And so it can, as Alberta, and the Drumheller region in particular, have yielded more than fifty species of dinosaur fossils.

THE FOSSIL BEDS

High in the Rocky Mountains, near the railway community of Field, British Columbia, rare fossils were first noticed in 1884 by CPR rail workers, who simply called them "stone bugs." What they were looking at were slabs of shale that had slipped from their formation higher up the mountainside.

In 1908 Charles Walcott of the Smithsonian Institute in Washington, D.C., decided to investigate

The stunning badlands of Alberta's Dinosaur Provincial Park, a World Heritage Site near Drumheller, Alberta, have yielded some of the world's rarest and most numerous dinosaur fossils.

this intriguing find and located the shale-bearing fossil formations high up Mount Stephen. Here, he excavated a quarry and discovered one of the most complete fossil sites the world had yet seen. What lay before his eyes was a five-hundred-million-year-old marine ecosystem that incredibly included both soft and hard marine tissues, many of them immaculately preserved.

Among the many species, the site includes sponges, brachiopods, trilobites, and the ancient predator *Anomalocaris canadensis*. The CPR jumped on the opportunity to promote the site, listing trilobites in its 1910 promotional guide, "The Challenge of the Mountains," as one of the area's tourist attractions.

Because of the rarity of its fossils, the Walcott Quarry is a guarded secret and not open to casual trekkers. Rather, the curious may engage in a tour led by a guide with the Burgess Shale Geoscience Foundation. Tours begin at the Yoho Trading Post in Field and are limited to twelve participants. The twenty-two-kilometre hike rises 825 metres, a challenging trek appropriate for only the fittest. Parks Canada guides will take hikers on a much shorter eight-kilometre stroll to see the lower shale beds, a hike that rises 795 metres.

The Burgess Shale, however, does not hold a monopoly on world-famous fossil finds. On the far opposite side of the country lie other treasure troves of remarkable ancient remains. One, known as the Miguasha fossils, first came to light in 1842 when Dr. Abraham Gesner of the Geological Survey of New Brunswick was probing a line of cliffs on the north side of the Baie-des-Chaleurs in Quebec. In 1879 the international community of scientists finally came to pay attention, and over the following decades exploration of the find took place.

The fossils are locked into the sandstones and shales of an ancient delta formed 380 million years ago. The finds include many early ancestors of today's fish species as well as long-extinct species, such as the heavily armoured placoderms, spiny acanthodians, and a few metre-long scorpions.

The province of Quebec opened a museum at the site in 1978 and then created a provincial park in 1985. UNESCO inscribed the location as a World Heritage Site in 1999.

In the mid-1800s a paleontologist named Charles Liddel discovered in the cliffs on the upper reaches of the Bay of Fundy a forest of fossilized trees, declaring it the "most wonderful phenomenon that I have seen." Today the Joggins fossils (from the Mi'kmaq term *chegoggins* or the "place of the big fish") are considered to be among the most important fossil locations on the planet. The fossilized trees here date back to the coal age, more than one hundred million years before the dinosaurs started roaming the earth. Trees here grew up to thirty metres in height. Embedded within one of those trees lie the fossilized remains of the *Hylonomus lyelli*, the oldest known land-dwelling reptile on the fossil record.

Stretching for several kilometres along the Bay of Fundy, the twelve-metre-high cliffs are continually eroded by the bay's famously high tides, exposing the flora and fauna of a complete rainforest ecosystem. The cliffs and its fossils were designated a UNESCO World Heritage Site in 2008.

In Newfoundland and Labrador, a seventeen-kilometre stretch of rugged, rocky coastline at Mistaken Point offers up the oldest known collection of multicellular fossils ever recorded, a treasure trove of ancient history that dates back 580 million years. Now part of the Mistaken Point Ecological Reserve, this fossil find became yet another Canadian UNESCO World Heritage Site in 2016.

SEVEN

WATER, WATER, EVERYWHERE:
CANADA'S GREATEST LAKES

Canada not only shares the world's largest freshwater lakes, the Great Lakes, but also claims the largest number of lakes on earth: 31,752, all being larger than three square kilometres. Of those, 561 are larger than a hundred square kilometres. Along with rivers and glaciers, they account for 9 percent of the world's freshwater supply.

THE GREAT LAKES

Even though Canada shares four of the five Great Lakes with the United States, Lakes Superior, Huron, Erie, and Ontario still rank among the top ten largest lakes in the country. Yet, it may come as a surprise that both Great Bear Lake and Great Slave Lake are larger in area than the Canadian portions of both Lake Ontario and Lake Erie. Water entering and flowing out of Lake Superior and Great Bear Lake requires 120 to 130 years to replenish.

However, it is the Great Lakes that are most widely known and most frequently visited. Their shores contain more than a quarter of Canada's population and many of its most scenic wonders as well.

Each of these immense water bodies offers its own distinctive geographic personality. The postglacial lagoons of the western end of Lake Ontario, attributed to the land rebounding at the east end of the lake following the retreat of the glaciers, have become the protected habitats of many plant and wildlife ecosystems. Those such as the Humber Marshes, the Rouge River in Canada's only national urban park, and Cootes Paradise, now part of the Royal Botanical Garden in Burlington, rank among the lake's most environmentally significant sites and are widely recognized. The massive sand dunes of Prince Edward County, its unusual Lake on the Mountain, which sits atop the brink of a hundred-metre-high limestone cliff, and the looming Scarborough Bluffs are also among Lake Ontario's geographical wonders.

Point Pelee in Lake Erie stabs like a pencil point into the lake's waters, making it the most southerly point of mainland Canada, located at a latitude south of northern California. Point Pelee is on the migratory route of the colourful monarch butterfly, and it hosts Carolinian vegetation and prickly pear cactus habitats.

Although out of bounds to the public, the largely privately owned Long Point in Lake Erie is a migratory bird route and now a UNESCO World Biosphere

The ever-changing sand spit in Point Pelee National Park is the most southerly point of mainland Canada.

Reserve. Extending eighteen kilometres into Lake Erie, it has been the scene of hundreds of shipwrecks, giving it the label "Canada's Lake Erie quadrangle." While the inner third of the point is overrun with cottages, marinas, and permanent homes, the outer third is now administered by the Canadian Wildlife Service and is off limits to the public, as is the middle third, which remains the private domain of an exclusive American hunting and fishing club.

Since 1793 Lake Erie has reputedly been the haven of a sea monster named Bessie, said to be a serpent-like creature fifteen metres long. Scientists have stated that the sightings were simply of large sturgeons. Nonetheless, the legend has given a local hockey team its name: the Lake Erie Monsters.

Lake Erie has spawned more than monsters. It is home to the world's largest freshwater fishing fleet, which harvests perch and pickerel. Due to extensive pollution on the American side of the lake, most commercial fishing takes place in Canadian waters. While Port Dover could until recently claim to be home to the world's largest freshwater fishing fleet, numbering more than seventy-five trawlers, most of those licences have been moved to the west end of the lake, with the fleets now concentrated in Wheatley and Erieau.

Dividing the waters of Lake Huron from those of Georgian Bay, the Bruce Peninsula, with its soaring limestone cliffs, is part of the Niagara Escarpment World Biosphere Reserve and is popular with hikers and divers alike. As with Long Point, it, too, has been the scene of hundreds of shipwrecks.

The north end of Lake Huron features Manitoulin Island, the world's largest freshwater island, connected to the mainland by only an ancient railway swing bridge. Overlooking the waters of the lake's North Channel are the white quartzite domes of the La Cloche Mountains, home to the sacred First Nations' spiritual promontory known as Dreamer's Rock and a popular subject for Canada's renowned Group of Seven artists.

Lake Superior is notorious for its ocean-sized waves like those that sank the SS *Edmund Fitzgerald* in a vicious storm in November 1975, taking its crew of twenty-nine with it. Meanwhile, the lake's massive red rock cliffs and ancient mountains that dominate its north shores have long attracted artists such as Lawren Harris and other members of the famous Group of Seven artists' collective. Superior's most prominent rock formation is the legendary Sleeping Giant. Said to be the resting form of Nanabijou, who was turned to stone when he revealed to European prospectors the site of a secret Anishinaabe silver deposit, its cliffs rise more than 240 metres above the tossing waters of the lake. It was voted one of Canada's "seven wonders" in a CBC audience competition.

The Sleeping Giant is an island located in Lake Superior, near Thunder Bay, Ontario. The island gets its name from the profile of the island's hills, which resemble a sleeping figure.

Human wonders abound along these lakes as well and include the Welland Canal, which links Lake Ontario with Lake Erie and whose builders had to find a way to conquer the limestone cliffs of the Niagara Escarpment. They have done so with the engineering marvel known as the twin flight locks, where massive freighters can lock through in both directions simultaneously in a trio of paired locks that flow into each other.

The Canadian locks at Sault Ste. Marie, while modest, now form part of a National Historic Site and allow only recreational vessels, while the commercial freighter traffic uses the larger and more modern locks on the U.S. side.

Remnants of failed industry abound as well, and the area has a legacy of ghost towns, such as the grain port of Depot Harbour on Georgian Bay, once the busiest on the Great Lakes, and Jackfish on Lake Superior, a former fishing centre and CPR coal dock operation. Both are now utterly abandoned.

While Indigenous lifestyles were largely transitory, the early inhabitants left their mark with the much-visited Agawa Rock Pictographs at Lake Superior Provincial Park and the strange Pukaskwa stone pits on the remote, rugged shores of Pukaskwa National Park. Large Anishinaabe nations remain on Manitoulin Island, where the Wikwemikong First Nation reserve remains the largest area of unceded land in Ontario.

With their long history of shipping, the Great Lakes also offer many of Canada's most historic lighthouses. Although they may be architecturally more modest than their American counterparts, they nonetheless recount the shipping legacy of these lakes. Most are simple square wooden towers, many of them now decommissioned. Others are more elaborate, such as the art deco concrete tower at Point Abino on Lake Erie. Although it is a National Historic Site, the cottage owners who own the road to it have, regrettably, opted to restrict access by "outsiders."

Among the oldest of Canada's Great Lakes lighthouses is that at Gibraltar Point on the Toronto Islands. At the time of its construction in 1808, it stood on the point, but since then, sand deposited from the easterly currents have extended the point farther into the lake, leaving the structure somewhat inland. The stone tower is said to be haunted by the ghost of its first keeper, John Rademuller, an illicit rum dealer who, it is said, failed to deliver a supply to the soldiers at nearby Fort York and was murdered for it. Bones later unearthed are believed to be his.

Another of the lake's oldest towers is the 1838 lighthouse that guards the entrance to Hamilton Harbour. On Lake Erie, the wooden light tower on the main street of Port Burwell is the Great Lakes' oldest wooden light tower, dating from 1842. Here, the adventurous can walk the narrow circular staircase to the light.

Georgian Bay and Lake Huron are home to Imperial Tower lighthouses such as those at Point Clark, a National Historic Site, and Chantry Island near Southampton, with their circular stone towers rising high into the air. Historic wooden lighthouses at Wingfield Basin on the Bruce Peninsula and Meldrum Bay on Manitoulin Island are now both museums.

While Georgian Bay's many mill towns have largely gone, heritage lighthouses still guide adventurous boaters through the dangerous labyrinth of rocks and shoals. The squat concrete form of the Red Rock lighthouse stands ten kilometres offshore, built in 1911 to replace earlier structures that were victims of the pounding waves that the bay can whip up. Most other early lighthouses have been replaced with steel frames with an autorotated light on top. The wooden lighthouse at Pointe au Baril, with its white wooden keeper's house and tapering wooden tower, is now privately owned. That which guards the entrance to Snug Harbour has the light tower rising from the roof of the former keeper's house.

CANADA'S WESTERN WATERS

Far to the west, many of the CPR's earliest postcards of its Rocky Mountain empire illustrate what are considered the country's most scenic lakes. Not too surprisingly, most are in the UNESCO Rocky Mountain Parks World Heritage Site.

Among them, Lake Louise is wildly popular with the tour bus crowd, with its distant glacier hanging over its turquoise water. Waterton Lake, in the park of the same name, provides the scenic backdrop for the views from the Prince of Wales Hotel, although it is notorious for its winds. The green-blue water of the isolated and little-known Berg Lake in Mount Robson Park (also part of the UNESCO Heritage Site) offers the tranquility of limited access. Similarly, Peyto Lake in the Waputik Range Valley of Banff National Park, at 1,860 metres above mean sea level, is popular with hikers and campers due to its stunning mountainous shores and distance from the crowds.

One of the world's most recognizable lakes is the much-photographed Moraine Lake. Since the CPR began featuring it on its early postcards, it has drawn tourists due largely to its backdrop of the Ten Peaks Mountains and its vibrant blues. The blue hues of many of these mountain lakes are attributed to the "glacial flour" in the waters that cascades from the many glaciers in the mountains.

Canada's lakes, too, have their share of oddities, such as a "disappearing" lake. That would be Medicine Lake in Alberta, where each spring and summer meltwaters from the icefields fill the lake basin, while in the fall, when the inflow stops, the waters drain out through sinkholes in the porous limestone bedrock.

Spotted Lake in British Columbia is often considered one of the world's oddest lakes. Although it contains little water, the many mineral deposits give it a spotted appearance.

Because Little Manitou Lake in Saskatchewan contains three times the salt concentration of the ocean, it has earned the name Canada's Dead Sea.

COTTAGE COUNTRY

While most of Canada's lakes remain remote, those closer to Canada's cities have historically been the best known and the most popular. And that perfectly describes Ontario's legendary Muskoka Lakes.

The main Muskoka Lakes consist of three interconnected lakes: Muskoka, Joseph, and Rosseau. With their lake levels raised during logging and steamer days, they were linked by means of small canals and locks at Port Carling, which links Muskoka and Rosseau, and Port Sandhurst, connecting Joseph and Rosseau. Countless other smaller lakes also make up the Muskoka Lakes region.

Their history, however, predates the steamer days. Until the 1860s the area known as the Ottawa-Huron Tract, those forested rock lands of the Canadian Shield between the Ottawa River and Georgian Bay, were the realm of the lumber barons. Throughout the region, lake levels were raised to facilitate the floating of the massive log booms to the sawmills throughout that area.

Then, as the forests were stripped by the loggers, the government opened the region to farming in 1868, offering free land along a series of "colonization roads." When the soil proved useless, most of the settlers followed the railways westward to the Prairie provinces, leaving behind them a landscape of abandoned farms and ghost towns.

Although the railways drew away the settlers, they also began to bring in the tourists. Drawn by the rocky scenery of the many lakes, people began to build resorts and small summer cabins in the area. By 1877 a fleet of steamers had begun shuttling the tourists from rail-side wharfs in Huntsville, Gravenhurst, and Bala to the new lodges and inns. By 1879 more than thirty resorts had opened, drawing vacationers from the heat and smog of the growing cities.

One other chain of lakes in Muskoka enjoyed steamer service and canal links, namely Mary Lake, Peninsula Lake, and Fairy Lake, all in the Huntsville area. A final link between Peninsula Lake and Lake of Bays, with its popular resorts, such as Bigwin Inn, was completed by the five-kilometre-long Huntsville and Lake of Bays "Portage" Railway, which operated from 1904 to 1959. Long after the sale of its steam and diesel locomotives, the Huntsville and Lake of Bays Railway Society brought the railway back "home" in 1984, restoring the equipment and now offering tourists a ride from a new station in Huntsville's Memorial Park to a small station on Fairy Lake.

By the 1950s the popularity of cottages was taking over from the resorts, and the auto age had made the railways and steamers obsolete; the last regular steamer made its final run in 1958. Since then many of these once-busy resort destinations have burned down or been converted to all-season destinations, or, more likely, condos.

The elegant Victorian style of the wooden twin-towered Windermere House (replicated exactly after 1996 when a movie crew working on *The Long Kiss Goodnight* caused a massive blaze that destroyed the original structure) recalls the beauty of the early lodges. All-season condos of the luxurious Deerhurst Resort, site of the controversial G20 Summit of 2010, and the Taboo Resort at Gravenhurst are the new incarnation of other early resorts and are highly sought after by visitors from around the world.

In 2012 the Ontario government ended the last of the rail service to the area when it shut down the historic Northlander train, a move that ignored the needs of not just vacationers but also residents living between Toronto and Cochrane.

However, there is still steamer service on the lakes. Departing from a replica railway station on the busy Gravenhurst wharf, the RMS *Segwun*, built in 1887 and painstakingly restored in 1981, puffs off in a cloud of genuine coal smoke on dinner, lunch, and sunset cruises around the three main Muskoka Lakes. A replica steamer, the *Wenonah II*, joined the fleet in 2002.

Many of the old family summer cottages have been replaced by the massive mansions of Millionaires' Row, a narrow channel in Lake Muskoka near Bracebridge, where even the boathouses are larger than many family homes elsewhere.

Wealthy American industrialists and Hollywood legends alike have found their "Golden Pond" in Muskoka. The Labatt, Bronfman, and Eaton families have all created grand summer estates on these shores. Hollywood, too, has discovered this wooded wilderness, a region that the *New York Times* has labelled the Malibu of the North. Goldie Hawn and Kurt Russell purchased their summer home on Lake Rosseau, as did their neighbour Martin Short. A visitor to the Muskoka Lakes may also encounter Steven Spielberg, Kate Hudson, and even Tom Hanks.

Yet, despite the excesses of the largest Muskoka Lakes, hundreds of smaller lakes around the regions

Built in 1887, the RMS *Segwun* (left) is North America's oldest operating steamship, offering regular excursions from Gravenhurst, Ontario. On the right, the *Wenonah II* is a more recent replication of an early Muskoka steamer.

of Muskoka, Parry Sound, and Haliburton still echo to the summer sounds of family fun. In fact, *National Geographic Traveler* has named Muskoka the world's number one summer travel destination.

NORTHERN LAKES

Canada's pristine and remote northern lakes attract fishers from around the world for week-long fly-in fishing trips, bringing needed benefits to the scattered First Nations Peoples that supply many of the guides.

Lakes such as Great Slave Lake and Great Bear Lake in the Northwest Territories provide sustenance to the First Nations Peoples and Inuit who depend on them, many of which provided early passage for explorers to the Arctic regions of the country and supplies of fur to the ubiquitous Hudson's Bay Company fur-trading posts.

While Canada's waterways remain among the cleanest on earth, climate change and ongoing issues with pollution mean that continuous monitoring and regulating is needed to keep them that way. No longer will the spectacle of Cleveland's Cuyahoga River catching fire due to its chemical content, as it did in the infamous episode in 1969, nor the mercury contamination of the English-Wabigoon River system in northwestern Ontario due to pollution from a single pulp mill in Dryden, be tolerated. Water is humankind's lifeblood. Without it, life could not exist, and Canada's lakes are a key component of that watery ecosystem.

EIGHT

GROUP OF SEVEN COUNTRY:
CANADA'S THIRTY THOUSAND ISLANDS BIOSPHERE RESERVE

Described as the world's most extensive freshwater archipelago, the Thirty Thousand Islands of Georgian Bay became inscribed as a UNESCO World Biosphere Reserve in 2004. Stretching from the resort community of Honey Harbour in the south for more than two hundred kilometres to the largely uninhabited French River mouth in the north, the island maze likely has more than a hundred thousand islands and shoals spread over its more than 347,000 square kilometres.

Islands range in size from Parry Island (seventy-two square kilometres) and Beausoleil Island (fourteen square kilometres) to small piles of bare rock with perhaps a tree or shrub to confirm their "island" status, but few rise more than a few metres over the bay's tossing waters.

As far back as two billion years ago, these rocks were part of an ancient mountain chain that geologists estimate rose as high the Himalayas do today. But millions of years of wind, water, and glaciers ground them down to the rounded rocky roots that linger today.

The mountain remnants received their final polish when the glaciers of the last ice age scoured them into rounded whaleback shoals and islands.

With the rising waters from the melting of those glaciers, waves washed them clean of most soils and sediments. They are said to be the oldest rocks on the earth's surface.

The Hurons or Wendat settled along the southern shores and the Anishinaabe along the eastern and northern shores. The Wendat took advantage of the more fertile soils to adopt a more sedentary lifestyle, using a rotating crop system, while the Anishinaabe remained nomadic, using the islands and shoals to seek food and sheltered passage.

The Wendat were attacked in 1649 by Haudenosaunee from what is today New York State. The Wendat dispersed and, other than the reconstructed Jesuit mission of Sainte-Marie among the Hurons, have left little visible legacy.

The Anishinaabe continue to occupy lands along the eastern shore, particularly the Magnetawan First Nation near the mouth of the Magnetawan River, the Beausoleil First Nation on Christian Island, and the Wasauksing First Nation on Parry Island.

The maze of islands and shoals proved an enormous hazard to boat traffic and to the first surveyors who tried to navigate them. Although the first European to see these waters was Samuel de Champlain in the early 1600s, not until 1819 did Lieutenant Henry Bayfield embark on a survey of the complex. The treacherous waters of the open bay, the lack of fertile land, and, of course, the challenges to navigation kept settlement at bay.

The lure of the lush pine forests that lay inland gradually drew industry to the bay. Lumber mills appeared at the mouths of the larger rivers, most notably at Muskoka Mills at the mouth of the Muskosh River, Copananing or French River Village on one of the many channels of the French River mouth, and Byng Inlet at the mouth of the Magnetawan River, where Holland and Graves erected what at the time was Canada's second-largest sawmill.

With the abundance of fish, small summer fishing villages occupied the more sheltered outer islands, such as the Mink, McCoy, and Bustard Islands. Fishing tugs operated by the large fishing companies would make the rounds of the colonies to gather up the catch and transport it to market.

Mill operators and fishers did not easily coexist. The fishers had long complained that the sawdust from the mills was destroying fish spawning areas, and finally in 1884 the Ontario government fined the Muskoka Mills owners over its extensive sawdust pollution. Evidence of that pollution remains evident today in the shallow waters of the river mouth.

Meanwhile, as the railways reached the southern shores of Georgian Bay, tourists began to realize the beauty and the bounty of the many picturesque islands, and a string of resort lodges appeared. The Copperhead, the Franceville, the Minnicog

on Minnicognashene Island, the Whalen Island Summer House, and the Sans Souci Hotel were all located south of Parry Sound, while the Ojibway Hotel was built near Byng Inlet to the north.

The beauty of the area, with its rugged rocks, crashing waves, and wind-bent pines, also attracted such Group of Seven painters as Arthur Lismer and Tom Thomson (who died before the group was actually formed).

Throughout this period, road access remained nearly nonexistent. A rough colonization road had made its way in the 1860s to the sheltered harbour that is today Parry Sound, and a small community grew around the mills and docks at this location.

The first railway to penetrate the shores of the Thirty Thousand Islands was known as the Ottawa, Arnprior and Parry Sound Railway, built by lumberman John Rudolphus Booth in 1895 from his Ottawa mills through Algonquin Park to the shores of Georgian Bay.

Forced to bypass Parry Sound, as the railway's original charter required, Booth instead created an entire new townsite on nearby Parry Island, naming it Depot Harbour. The townsite grew to include more than a hundred houses, along with hotels, churches, schools, two massive grain elevators, a coal dock, and railway yards complete with concrete roundhouse.

The grain port remained one of Georgian Bay's busiest until the mid-1930s, when a bridge that carried the tracks through Algonquin Park was damaged, severing the railway's lifeline. The grain elevators burned a decade later, and Depot Harbour became one of Ontario's largest ghost towns. The buildings were eventually disassembled and removed, or burned, in the succeeding years. The only evidence of the town's existence today is the shell of the railway roundhouse, along with the sidewalks and concrete foundations of the many houses, now heavily overgrown. The Canadian Northern and Canadian Pacific Railways entered Parry Sound from the south more than a decade later, and their lines remain in use.

Parry Sound had begun as a rowdy colonization road terminus named Codrington. Later, William Beatty erected a sawmill and laid out a new townsite (which he declared would be alcohol-free), and, with its deep and protected harbour, Parry Sound became the urban and industrial hub of the archipelago.

Near the mouth of the French River, the Canadian Northern Railway extended a branch from its main line to the mouth of the Key Inlet at Key Harbour, transhipping iron ore pellets from Sudbury's Moose Mountain mine onto freighters bound for U.S. ports. The place also contained a powerhouse and coal dock along with a railway bunkhouse.

The transhipment operation was subsequently moved to the large docks in Depot Harbour. Today Key Harbour contains the ruins of the powerhouse and the cribbing from the coal dock and now functions primarily as a popular fishing camp.

The ghost town of Depot Harbour is tucked in among the Thirty Thousand Islands of Georgian Bay. Once a prosperous port and railway terminus, the town began to decline in the 1930s, and by the late 1950s had been completely abandoned. Today, only a few foundations, sidewalks, stone steps, and the Roman-like ruin of the railway roundhouse, shown here, are to be found.

Road links to the south, however, still remained years away, and tourists continued to arrive by rail and steamer to vacation in the many lodges. By then many of the pine stands that supplied the lumber mills were depleted, and those operations moved inland to be closer to the railway lines. Workers' villages were demolished, larger communities like French River Village and Muskoka Mills disappearing entirely, while Byng Inlet never recovered from a disastrous fire in the mills and remains a fraction of its original size. With the advent of large, enclosed fishing tugs, the fishers moved their home base to larger rail-side harbours like Midland, Collingwood, and Thornbury. As they did, the summer fishing colonies were abandoned, leaving scant evidence of their existence.

By the 1920s early roads had made their way as far as Honey Harbour, where the islands' first cottage community began; some structures from that period still survive today.

By the 1960s highways had been blasted through the tough granite rocks to reach Parry Sound, and the convenience of car and cottage replaced the weary old lodges. (One infamous blast dislodged more than a hundred rattlesnakes.) The sole surviving island lodge today is the Ojibway, which still welcomes guests who enjoy the lodge life on the outer islands.

Inevitably, Ontarians soon began to worry about the fate of this natural wonder, especially with the boom in cottages and summer homes. In response, in 1929 the government of Canada established the Georgian Bay Islands National Park based on Beausoleil Island at the south end of the archipelago along with forty small outer islands. Campers and hikers can access the Beausoleil Island by a shuttle launch from the docks in Honey Harbour.

To further protect the islands, in the 1970s the Ontario government established the Massasauga Provincial Park, an extensive area of islands extending from the mouth of the Moon River northward to Parry Island. Its many remote island campsites attract motorboaters, canoers, and kayakers.

Among these islands lies the wreck of the doomed steamer the *Waubuno*, which capsized and sank in a raging snowstorm in 1879 and whose hull lies just beneath the surface of the water adjacent to the aptly named Wreck Island. But the mystery remains as to the whereabouts of the superstructure, and no bodies were ever recovered.

Killbear Provincial Park, a short distance from Parry Sound, with its beaches, campsites, views across the waters of the bay, and road access, has become one of the province's most popular park destinations. Reservations for campsites are often made a year in advance.

In 1998 the Georgian Bay Islands Biosphere was incorporated and began lobbying for the area's inscription as a UNESCO World Biosphere Reserve, which they achieved just six years later. Based in Parry Sound, the two-hundred-member Biosphere Action Group remains active in promoting sustainable development and sound conservation practices through such initiatives as "Grow Your Own Grub" and a Biosphere Camp. The reserve extends from Honey Harbour in the south to the French River in the north and as far inland as Lake Joseph.

The rugged beauty of the Thirty Thousand Islands attracted artists such as the Group of Seven and spawned its designation as a World Biosphere Reserve.

Most accommodations are based in Parry Sound (no longer alcohol-free), with its range of bed and breakfasts and hotel chains, and the town now serves as the busy hub of the entire eastern Georgian Bay region. VIA Rail stops at the town's two historic stations, although most visitors arrive by car. As there is no road access to view the outer islands, the town also offers the archipelago's only boat cruise on the *Island Queen*. A wide overview of the inner harbour can be had from the top of the fire tower in town.

NINE

THE FRONTENAC ARCH BIOSPHERE RESERVE

THE RESERVE

To the driver travelling east on Highway 401, the entry into the Frontenac Biosphere is evident enough, if one knows what to look for. Lying in a rock cut on the north side of the 401 at the Highway 15 exit ramp near Kingston lies a five-hundred-million-year gap in Ontario's geological history. In this rock cut, a layer of flat grey limestone is perched on top of a mound of pink granite, the eroded remnants of a massive mountain range half a billion years older.

Once as high as today's Rocky Mountains, these ancient rocks were gradually worn away by wind, water, ice, and time, turning them into rounded rocky knobs interspersed with river valleys, lakes, ponds, and swamps. When the region was submerged in a tropical sea, sand and silt settled to the bottom to harden and become layers of limestone resting above the old mountain roots, which are known today as the Canadian Shield.

While the ancient shield rocks encompass most of northern Canada, here in eastern Ontario, those rocks extend southward to link with the equally aged rocks of the Appalachian Mountains in New York State. Geologists have labelled this link the Frontenac Axis. (Frontenac is the name of the local county.)

With the ending of the last ice age, estimated at twenty thousand years ago, the waters of a postglacial Lake Ontario began to flow eastward around those rock knobs, creating the Thousand Islands.

The region also forms the intersection of five major forest regions, including the boreal and the Appalachian forest regions. Archaeological evidence indicates that early Indigenous Peoples converged on the region from all directions to trade in shells, metals, and furs.

This intersection of river and rock created a natural intersection for human activity and animal movement, a rare juxtaposition that has earned its status as the Frontenac Arch UNESCO World Biosphere Reserve (or the FAB, as locals refer to it).

The FAB covers some 2,700 square kilometres and extends roughly from Brockville in the southeast to Frontenac Provincial Park in the northwest. Along the St. Lawrence River, the FAB extends from Brockville to Gananoque. Within this region, under UNESCO's stipulations, it is the role of governments at all levels, volunteer groups, and the private sector to encourage environmental education and sustainable development that respects the natural and cultural attributes of this special region.

Opportunities abound for visitors to engage in the FAB's natural attractions. Provincial parks include the Charleston Lake Provincial Park and the Frontenac Provincial Park, where the many trails lead along rugged shorelines, over granite knobs, and past the sites of failed farmsteads and forgotten mines. Here, too, one may encounter Canada's largest snake, the rat snake, which can grow to nearly three metres (although legend has it that an early farmer killed a five-metre-long specimen).

Boat tours depart from wharfs in Gananoque, Ivy Lea, and Rockport to allow visitors to tour the scenic shores of the Thousand Islands and gape at the extravagance of their summer palaces, like that of Boldt Castle, while the Thousand Islands Parkway, which connects Gananoque with Brockville, offers drivers and cyclists vistas of the river and islands from the shore.

Even rail travellers on VIA Rail's Toronto–Montreal and Toronto–Ottawa routes enjoy unobstructed views of nature's backyard that motorists may miss.

Hikers can follow any of several trails that cross the reserve. The 387-kilometre Rideau Trail generally

Boldt Castle in the Thousand Islands of the St. Lawrence River recalls the days when American millionaires erected grand summer homes on the islands and shorelines along what is known as Millionaires' Row.

follows the Rideau Canal and its tributary waterways from Kingston to Ottawa, leading through many areas of rocky wilderness, while the Cataraqui Trail follows the former Canadian Northern Rail bed from Napanee to Smiths Falls. The Kingston and Pembroke Rail Trail passes through the reserve and leads north from Kingston to Renfrew. Boaters wishing to view the reserve from the water can choose to cruise either the St. Lawrence River or the Rideau Canal (itself a UNESCO World Heritage Site).

Urban sprawl has yet to creep into the area's hinterlands, leaving the region an escape from the tedium of the Ottawas and Torontos (and, sadly, even the Kingstons) of our modern urban age.

The FAB was created in 2002 and is headquartered in Lansdowne, Ontario, where information brochures are available, but the tourism hub is undoubtedly the riverside town of Gananoque, with its many historic buildings, summer theatre, and one of the embarkation points to the popular Thousand Islands cruises.

The Thousand Islands

The most dramatic manifestation of the FAB is the stunning Thousand Islands, where the pink granite knobs of the Frontenac Axis peer through the waters of the St. Lawrence River.

Once the glaciers had receded from the eastern end of a higher postglacial Lake Ontario, the waters began to swirl through the rocky knobs of the uplifted arch, creating the rocky maze of the Thousand Islands. The true number of islands is more like 1,800, depending on which definition of an island is used. Some definitions require the rock to have at least two trees and be permanently above the water. Other definitions are content with just a single tree.

The archipelago begins with Wolfe Island at Lake Ontario's outlet near Kingston (although being a more recent limestone mass, Wolfe Island is not part of the more ancient Frontenac Axis geological feature) and extends east to Brockville.

The first explorers of the region were the Haudenosaunee, who named the area Manitouana, meaning "the garden of the great spirit." Archaeological evidence of various trade goods confirms that First Nations Peoples used the island chain as a cultural axis. That all ended with the arrival of the first of the European invaders, Jacques Cartier, in 1535, and the start of the many Iroquois Wars. A little over a century later, surveyor Jean Desbayes named the outcrops Les Milles-Îles, or Thousand Islands.

The islands became the focus of decades of hostilities: the French versus the Haudenosaunee, the British versus the French, the British versus the Americans, and then the British versus William Lyon Mackenzie's Upper Canada rebels.

The islands were even the hangout of a so-called pirate named Bill Johnson, a Kingstonian who used his schooners to smuggle tea and rum across the watery border. During the 1838 rebellion against the entrenched British political establishment in Upper Canada, launched by William Lyon Mackenzie, a former mayor of Toronto, Johnson sided with the rebel faction. Assigned by Mackenzie to the Thousand Islands region, Johnson transported an armed group to Wellesley Island, where they captured and burned the vessel *Sir Robert Peel*. While members of his brigade were arrested (and eventually acquitted), Johnson remained at large, hiding out among the Thousand Islands, which, thanks to his rum-running days, he knew intimately.

Later in 1838 he was at it again, ferrying men and supplies across the river to attack the British at Prescott. In the Battle of Windmill Point (now a National Historic Site near Prescott), the rebel force was defeated, and Johnson surrendered to the Americans. He spent little time in jail and died while living in his son's hotel in Clayton, New York, in 1853. His legacy lives on in the annual Bill Johnson Pirate Days held in Alexandria Bay, New York.

A tiny cottage amid the Thousand Islands of the St. Lawrence River is in stark contrast to the grand summer palaces of Millionaires' Row.

Aside from Johnson's activities, the Thousand Islands remained peaceful. The U.S.-Canada boundary, established in 1783 following the American Revolution, zig-zags through the island chain, careful to not cross any island and to remain at least thirty-three metres from any portion of the mainland.

The railways hastened the arrival of wealthy American industrialists seeking vacation property in this scenic island region. Here, they erected some of North America's grandest summer homes during an era known as the Golden Age, which lasted from 1888 to 1905.

Among them is the massive stone structure known as Boldt Castle, erected in 1900 by George Boldt, owner of the Waldorf Astoria Hotel in New York City. It was intended for his wife, who, sadly, passed away before the structure was even completed. It has been immaculately restored to much of its former glory.

Another is the long-vacant Carleton Villa on Carleton Island near Cape Vincent. Built in 1895 by William Wyckoff, manufacturer of the Remington typewriter, who died a year later, it stands empty and vandalized, up for sale for several years.

Near Alexandria Bay on the New York side, Deer Island is owned by the curiously named and secretive Skull and Bones Society. On Cherry Island, part of the legendary Millionaires' Row, sits Casa Blanca, built in the late 1800s by the Pullman family of railway fame. Although privately owned, it is open to the public for tea.

One of the last castles of the Golden Age was the Towers on Dark Island near the eastern end of the island chain. It was built in 1902 for Frederick

Gilbert Bourne, manufacturer of the Singer sewing machine. Still prominent today, it now goes by the name Singer Castle.

By comparison, with fewer railway links, Canadian shores saw few millionaires. The Brockville and Ottawa Railway opened shipping through Brockville in the 1850s, while the Kingston and Pembroke Railway forged its lines north from the harbour at Kingston to Renfrew in the 1880s.

Gananoque finally received its rail link to the distant Grand Trunk Railway line with the opening of the Thousand Islands Railway in 1877, bringing tourists to such grand hotels as the Gananoque Inn, which continues to host visitors to the town. The nearby Thousand Islands Playhouse offers docks for theatregoers arriving by water. This waterside theatre is housed in the 1909 clubhouse of the former Gananoque Canoe Club.

While the tracks of the Thousand Islands Railway (TIR) have long since been removed and the harbour station burned down twenty years ago, the town's railway heritage is preserved with the 1930s diesel engine number 500 parked by the TIR's tiny "umbrella" station, a trackside shelter built in 1880 on the town's main street. (The nearest railway access today is the VIA station on the CN line about twelve kilometres north of the town, an attractive if diminutive depot styled after the towered Gananoque Inn.)

Besides the popular boat cruises, visitors can obtain an aerial view of the islands from the seat of a helicopter at Gananoque or from the 130-metre level of the Thousand Islands Tower on Hill Island near the U.S. border crossing.

Parks Canada administers the Thousand Islands National Park (also known as the St. Lawrence Islands National Park) with its twenty-four islands, trails, and campgrounds. The park office is located in Mallorytown Landing.

TEN

THE "AMAZON OF THE NORTH": CANADA'S GREAT BEAR RAINFOREST

On the northwest coast of British Columbia, a 450-kilometre stretch of the world's largest temperate rainforest was, until 1997, threatened with clear-cut logging. That is when the local First Nations Peoples, along with various environmental groups and just plain concerned citizens, began a call to action to save the forests.

By 2006 the effort began to pay off when the province of British Columbia declared five million hectares of old-growth timber off limits to logging. In 2016 Prince William and the Duchess of Cambridge endorsed the region under the Queen's Commonwealth Canopy Initiative, a designation that includes other sensitive forest covers in Singapore, New Zealand, New Guinea, Namibia, Saint Kitts, and Fiji.

Finally, on January 1, 2017, the B.C. government enacted the Great Bear Rainforest Act, protecting 85 percent of the world's largest intact temperate rainforest.

From Campbell River in the south, the forest extends to the head of Portland Canal north of Prince Rupert in the north and rises from the sea to the peaks of the jagged and ice-capped Coast Mountains, taking in 6.5 million hectares, or an area the size of Ireland.

The region is the domain of grizzly and black bears, cougars, Sitka deer, and mountain goats. Also found here is the rare and elusive Kermode bear. This white-coated animal is not a polar bear but rather a black bear with a recessive gene that gives it a white coat. To the Tsimshian First Nations, it is known as Moksg'mol, the sacred spirit bear; it earned its English name from Francis Kermode, who helped locate and identify the rare animal. Local First Nations Peoples have various cultural stories surrounding the spirit bear. One such story sees Raven creating the spirit bear as a reminder of the last ice age.

Within the rainforest, the Kitasoo Spirit Bear Conservancy is centred along Laredo Sound on Princess Royal Island, British Columbia's fourth-largest island. One of the chief reasons for establishing the conservancy is the protection of the Kermode bear, although it takes in a remarkable range of marine and other land-based species as well. Designated in 2006, the conservancy is co-managed by the B.C. government and the local Kitasoo/Xai'xais First Nation. In the conservancy's 103,000 hectares, a population of about 120 of the bears, out of 400 in all the rainforest, attracts visitors from around the globe, although not in vast numbers, as access is remote and pricey.

Great Bear Rainforest, also known as the Amazon of the North, is the last of the world's great temperate rainforests.

The town of Klemtu lies within the conservancy on Swindle Island, which is located in British Columbia's Inside Passage and requires two flights from the Vancouver airport plus an hour-and-a-half boat ride to reach. The Spirit Bear Lodge offers guided tours to the bear habitats. To discourage poaching, these locations are not publicized. The lodge is owned by the local Kitasoo/Xai'xais First Nation community.

As the name implies, the rainforest is as much about its trees as it is about the spirit bear. Here, western red cedars, which can date back more than a thousand years, have been the lifeblood of the many First Nations Peoples, providing them with clothing, shelter, baskets, totems, and transportation. The eighty watersheds in the forest area include 2,500 yearly salmon runs, providing both food and income for these nations.

Archaeologists have discovered hundreds of First Nations sites, many dating back ten thousand years, that include the remains of log houses, totems, and rock etchings known as petroglyphs.

European intrusions began with early fur-trading posts and then expanded to include sawmills and canneries, twenty of which appeared along Smith Inlet between 1882 and 1937. They are all silent now. Mining towns swept in, such as Anyox, which is now a ghost town, and Ocean Falls, which closed in 1982 but has begun to attract new residents.

Within the rainforest, the town of Bella Coola offers the only road access. Other communities are accessible by boat or float plane, many coming from Port Hardy or from Vancouver's International Airport, to Bella Coola, Bella Bella, or Klemtu. Gift shops in Bella Coola, such as the Petroglyph Gallery and the Museum of Northern British Columbia, offer visitors the opportunity to purchase local First Nations craftworks.

Today the community of Bella Bella, also known as Waglisla, has assumed the role of main centre for the water-bound communities, with a hospital, school, and airport. A number of remote lodges offer fishing and guided tours, such as the Nimmo Bay Resort, which generates its own electricity from a nearby waterfall. BC Ferries offers access via its Discovery Passage route. *National Geographic* has described the Discovery Passage as one of the world's "top trips."

In his prelude to the wonderful picture book on the rainforest titled *The Great Bear Rain Forest, Canada's Forgotten Coast* by Ian and Karen McAllister, Robert F. Kennedy Jr. wrote that here lies "one of nature's great masterpieces." Anyone who lives there, or visits, could not help but agree.

Besides the rainforest, Canada can claim other successes in its preservation efforts. In 2010 the Canadian Boreal Forest Agreement was signed by representatives of both the forest industry and conservation groups. Covering more than seventy-three million hectares of public forests, the agreement directly protects twenty-nine million hectares of boreal forest across the country.

Then, in November 2017, the Supreme Court of Canada ruled in favour of protecting the sixty-eight-thousand-square-kilometre Peel watershed in Yukon. The ruling would protect 80 percent of the watershed from development. The decision effectively

The unusual white-coated Kermode bear, known as the spirit bear, is one of the inhabitants of the Great Bear Rainforest.

negated a plan by the Yukon government that would save only 30 percent from exploitation. The court had harsh words for the Yukon government, stating that by ignoring the recommendations of an earlier planning commission, "Yukon's conduct was not becoming to the honour of the Crown."

Although uninhabited, the Peel watershed provides water, food, and natural medicines for the Tr'ondëk Hwëch'in First Nation and contains a wide range of fish, wildlife, and plant species.

Also in November 2017, Parks Canada announced the creation of the country's largest nature preserve. At 110,000 square kilometres, the Tallurutiup Imanga–Lancaster Sound National Marine Conservation Area takes in the main Lancaster Sound entrance to the fabled Northwest Passage. Extending from Clyde River on Baffin Island in the east, the area takes in Lancaster Sound and extends west to Resolute and as far north as Ellesmere Island. According to Parks Canada, the region is home to 75 percent of the world's narwhal population, 20 percent of Canada's belugas, and the country's largest subpopulation of polar bears. An estimated 3,600 Inuit also inhabit the area.

ELEVEN

PINGO! AND OTHER ARCTIC ODDITIES

It is unlikely that many Canadians have heard of a pingo, a geological landmark unique to northern regions. Large cone-shaped hills rising from a flat tundra plain, pingos develop over prolonged periods of time as water in a subsurface lake freezes, expands, and pushes upward, much like the bump in the centre of an ice cube, and they are only able to form in areas of permafrost. Over the years, the centre of a pingo may collapse, resulting in a volcano-type crater lake. Pingos typically form in former lake basins, on lower valley slopes, and on alluvial fans. They may range in height anywhere from five to fifty metres.

While pingos occur across the Arctic world, the largest concentration lies in Canada's Mackenzie Delta, where more than 1,400 pingos are known to exist. Other examples are found on Banks Island and Bylot Island as well as in other Arctic regions in Siberia, Greenland, and Alaska.

Pingos, which in Inuktitut means "small hill," were first documented by explorer John Richardson in his sketches of 1848. These depict two of the Arctic's largest pingos, which even have names: Ibyuk and Aklisuktuk.

The term was brought into use in the English language in 1938 by Alf Porsild, who, in fact, has one such hill named in his honour. (The scientific name for pingo is the somewhat less interesting "hydrolaccolith.")

The Ibyuk pingo measures fifty metres high and is an estimated one thousand years old. It continues to grow about two centimetres per year and forms part of Canada's only designated national landmark. The sixteen-square-kilometre Pingo National Landmark includes eight protected pingos and lies five kilometres west of Tuktoyaktuk. Established in 1984, the landmark is co-managed by the government of Canada and the Inuvialuit Land Administration.

The landmark is not entirely unknown. Scottish entertainer Jimmy Connolly has featured it in his televised geographic odyssey, *Journey to the Edge of the World.* The Spectacular Northwest Territories website refers to its pingos as "the North's weirdest secret."

To facilitate access, usually through local boat operators from Tuktoyaktuk, Parks Canada has added a wharf, boardwalk, viewing platforms, and interpretative signage.

Another strange Arctic phenomenon, tundra polygons, are often found in pingo territory and occur when water seeps into cracks in the ground to form ice wedges, which, when they connect with

The permafrost of the Canadian Arctic has heaved up icy mounds known as pingos, many of which lie within Parks Canada's Pingo National Landmark.

Located on the east coast of Cape Bathurst in the Northwest Territories, the Smoking Hills are literally on fire. They contain layers of oil shales that have been burning continuously for centuries.

each other, form polygonal formations in the tundra. Underground ice beds may occur in the tundra as well, some of which are five hundred metres long and ten metres high.

A trip into Franklin Bay reveals an unusual phenomenon known as the Smoking Hills. In these Arctic hillsides, a form of bituminous shale contains the volatile mineral known as jarosite, which ignites upon exposure to frigid air, resulting in continuous smoking.

To paraphrase the words of a poem by Yukon poet Robert Service, "The Cremation of Sam McGee," there are strange things found 'neath the midnight sun.

TWELVE

INUKSUIT:
THE STONE MEN OF THE ARCTIC

Across Canada's barren Arctic landscapes, men of stone beckon many a weary traveller, just as they have for centuries. These stone piles are known as inuksuit (or "inuksuk" in the singular) or more commonly anglicized to "inukshuks," translated as "likeness of men." Some of these figures may date back two thousand years, or roughly the time that Inuit ancestors, the Thule and Dorset Peoples, began to inhabit the brutal lands of Canada's North.

In this region, mere survival was a challenge. Early Inuit would erect human-like stone piles for several reasons. One was simply to provide direction. Visible for long distances across the treeless barrens, they allowed travellers to follow routes to game, shelter, or the next village. Others could be ceremonial, while still others might contain vital caches of meat, or possibly warn of danger, all depending on the configuration.

An inuksuk with arms raised might be a warning sign that the location may be dangerous, while one with a hole in it might mean that anyone who looks through it is shown the way ahead. In any event, the inuksuit were vital to survival in the Far North.

While many survive scattered across the barren lands of the Arctic, there is one prominent collection of roughly a hundred such structures in a concentrated area near Cape Dorset on Baffin Island. Set in two groups, some rise as high as 2.5 metres and have been attributed to the work of the Thule. Situated on the Foxe Peninsula, 88.5 kilometres from Cape Dorset, they are now protected in the Parks Canada Inuksuit National Historic Site, created in 1969.

The region also includes a variety of early Arctic heritage sites, including the wreck of the HMS *Breadalbane*, which sank in 1853 while seeking the fate of the doomed Franklin expedition. It, too, is a National Historic Site. Other surprising ruins include those of early Thule populations, Martin Frobisher's 1576 gold-mining site, and an 1857 whaling station.

Not all inuksuit are warmly received. Three such structures built at Toronto's Pearson International Airport were dismantled to allow for renovation of the terminal and then reassembled. But, according to the original Inuk builder, the restoration was inaccurate and disrespectful to his people. They were later reassembled correctly.

In 2015 residents of Goderich erected 150 stone inuksuit along the shore of Lake Huron, which began to attract curious tourists. However, after one visitor was injured while posing on one and threatened to

Although this inuksuk is found in Toronto, those scattered around the Arctic provided vital, life-saving information for Inuit travellers.

sue, the town's lawyers urged their removal, and a year later they were gone.

Drivers along Highway 69/400 in the Parry Sound area will find small inuksuit perched on the high rock cuts on the newly constructed section of the highway. Their purpose and origin is unclear, but they are unlikely the work of any local Inuit.

Others in southern Canada do offer legitimate significance. In Toronto, near Lake Ontario, Kelly Qimirpik, from Cape Dorset, created a giant ten-metre inuksuk with an arm span of five metres as a tribute to the 2002 World Youth Day. Located at Lakeshore Road and Newfoundland Road, it is considerably more accessible than those near Cape Dorset.

An inuksuk on the grounds of Rideau Hall in Ottawa is the work of Kananginak Pootoogook, who created it in 1997. High above Vancouver's English Bay looms a large inuksuk created by Nunavut's Alvin Kanak for the 1986 Vancouver World Exposition. Still another was erected on the Juno Beach site in France. The inuksuk also became the symbol of the Vancouver 2010 Winter Olympics, although some have labelled this as cultural appropriation.

Regardless of the location or the purpose, the stone men of the Arctic represent one of Canada's genuine, albeit unusual, international icons.

The flag of Nunavut prominently features an inuksuk.

THIRTEEN

THE WATCHERS:
CANADA'S WEST COAST TOTEMS

Perhaps the most iconic of Canada's West Coast images is not the nudists on Wreck Beach but rather the totem pole.

Records do not indicate when the first humans began arriving on the west coast of British Columbia, but it is clear that they were a sea-faring culture. Here, amid the coves of the jagged and mountainous coast, they established their villages.

Their lifeblood was the western red cedar. This sturdy species provided the inhabitants with nearly everything they needed: tools, transportation, housing, cooking vessels, even some clothing, and the totem poles.

British Columbia is home to 198 First Nations, about one-third of all First Nations in Canada, and has the greatest diversity of Indigenous cultures in Canada. Seven of Canada's eleven Indigenous language families are located exclusively in British Columbia, representing more than 60 percent of the country's First Nations languages. While most took up territory in British Columbia's interior, the Haida and the Tlingit were the main coastal groups, and it is here that their totem heritage is most evident.

The pole carvers used the logs, sometimes ten metres high, to tell their family story, to describe their heritage, or to serve as monuments and memorials for generations past and generations to come. The red cedar is largely resistant to rot and fungus; decay can only begin from the inside and work its way outward — a long, slow process. Unfortunately, in recent years that is what is coming to pass among the oldest of the poles.

Prior to the 1830s, thousands of the coastal people lived in hundreds of villages. They would trade, hold potlaches, and sometimes war among each other. Then the Europeans began to arrive. Along with the desired iron pots and prized weapons came the diseases, especially smallpox, which over the next half-century would decimate 90 percent of the First Nations population. In the vacated villages, the longhouses collapsed, while the massive war canoes rotted on the beaches. The only evidence left was the sturdy totems.

As time passed and the unique cultural significance of these memorials began to dawn on the non-Indigenous population of the country, museums and private collectors began to cart away the monumental poles. Others fell to the ground and rotted. Some became the subject of the famous paintings by Emily Carr, such as the *Totem Walk of the Sitka* (1907) and *Kitwancool* (1928), although some today might consider these renderings to be cultural appropriation.

Little wonder that the totems that still survive in their original locations have become invaluable heritage sites.

The most complete surviving examples of early on-site totems lie on the shores of the Haida Gwaii island of SG ang Gwaay in the village of Ninstints. Here stand the remains of twenty poles dating back more than two hundred years, some as high as six metres, along with the remains of several traditional longhouses.

Abandoned in the 1850s, the site today is described by UNESCO as "unique in the world" and one which "commemorates the living culture of the Haida people and their relation to the land and sea." In 1981 that body inscribed SGang Gwaay as a World Heritage Site.

Then, in 2004, that agency added the entire island archipelago of Gwaii Hanaas as a World Heritage Site, the same year in which the National Historic Sites and Monuments Board of Canada designated it a National Historic Site.

Within the 138-island archipelago lie more than six hundred significant Haida sites, including K'uuna Llnagaay, which contains many poles, as well as T'aanuu Llnagaay, which contain various village ruins.

Many of the sites lie under the watchful eyes of traditional Watchmen, elders who act as security guards, caretakers, and tour guides for the few visitors who manage to reach the sites. Access is not easy and usually requires individual watercraft, such as kayaks, or boats operated by local tour operators. There are no roads or airports in the sensitive sites.

Graham Island and Moresby Island are the only developed and easily accessible communities on the islands of Haida Gwaii, offering accommodation, restaurants, and the jumping-off points for the tours to the totems.

Throughout the twentieth century, the cultural value of the totems gained appreciation by a society that once regarded them as backward and to be removed along with most other Indigenous cultural practices.

Indeed, across the country, many have become cultural tourist attractions.

The most noteworthy of these is in Duncan, British Columbia. Situated on Vancouver Island's eastern shore, about two hours from Victoria, the city has dubbed itself City of Totems. In recognition of the city's intrinsic link with Indigenous culture, the mayor and city council in 1985 embarked on a consultation with the Cowichan Tribes Chiefs and engaged master carver Simon Charlie to mentor Indigenous carvers to tell their stories on the totems. Assisted with funding from the Department of Canadian Heritage, the carvers raised the poles one by one, all in keeping with traditional pole-raising ceremonies.

Today forty-one such monuments line the city streets, most clustered by the historic Esquimaux and Nanaimo railway station. When the VIA Rail trains still operated, tourists by the hundreds would disembark to follow a tour guide, or go off on their own, reading the plaques that tell the individual stories of the carvers. Today, with rail service suspended, it is the tour buses that crowd the city's streets.

While the totems of Duncan are of recent vintage, those clustered in Vancouver's Stanley Park originated from traditional totem sites, and many date back nearly

The ancient totems of the Gwaii Haanas on British Columbia's coastal islands, a UNESCO World Heritage Site, are considered one of the world's historic wonders.

a century. The nine poles currently situated in Brockton Point are, in fact, replicas and are replacement poles commissioned in the 1980s when most of the originals were sent off to various museums for preservation.

Toronto's Royal Ontario Museum offers four ancient poles for visitors to appreciate. They include crest poles carved by Nisga'a and Haida carvers and were acquired in the 1920s. The Pole of Sagaween, the tallest of the group at 24.5 metres, dates from the nineteenth century; the Three Persons Along, at 10 metres, dates from 1860; the Strong House Pole is from 1910; and the oldest is the Shaking Pole of Kw'axsuu, which was carved in the 1840s and rises 14 metres.

In Ottawa, the Canadian Museum of History presents the story of Canada's West Coast peoples with replicas of longhouses, artifacts, and the largest, albeit modern, indoor collection of totems, all created by Indigenous carvers. Vancouver's Museum of Anthropology displays poles and artifacts from a wide variety of British Columbia's First Nations cultures as well as poles carved by contemporary First Nations artists.

Kitwanga, which lies on the Yellowhead Highway 16 at the Stewart-Cassiar Crossing, contains fifty totems within an hour's drive, several of them dating back over a century. Nearby Kitwancool still contains more than twenty poles, although it could once claim Canada's largest pole assemblage. The Hole in the Sky totem is more than 140 years old.

In 2011 Jasper, Alberta, saw the carving and erection of the forty-seven-metre-high Two Brothers totem, which replaced a century-old Raven pole.

This totem pole in Stanley Park in Vancouver is one of a number of such works created by contemporary Indigenous artists located there.

The new pole was carved by brothers Jaalen and Gwaai Edenshaw.

Alert Bay on northern Vancouver Island contains what many claim to be, at 52.7 metres, the world's highest totem. Others dispute that claim, arguing that it is, in reality, two totems. The figures on it represent thirteen First Nations in that area. Alert Bay's memorial park contains several memorial totems. However, visitors are not permitted on those sacred grounds.

Trail Bay on Shíshálh First Nation territory on British Columbia's Sunshine Coast is home to a dozen totems that depict the animals of the various nations, including wolves, grizzlies, orcas, and eagles. A self-directed guide leads to the poles, most of which are fewer than thirty-five years old, and describes the significance of each.

One of the most striking tributes to the totem culture of Indigenous West Coast villages is that found in the Royal B.C. Museum in Victoria. Housed in its large quarters, the centrepiece of the museum's First Peoples gallery is the stunning Totem Hall, which was opened in 1977, though the museum has been preserving totems since 1913.

Upon walking into this two-storey hall, visitors are confronted with a forest of totems, most dating back more than a century. These include crest poles, house posts, and mortuary poles, where the remains of chiefs were laid in boxes atop the post. On display is a house post, which contains a hole through which to enter the home.

Beyond the hall, visitors enter a space created by Chief Jonathan Hunt that acts both as a museum exhibit and a ceremonial place. On the grounds outside the museum is Thunderbird Park, established in 1941, which contains several poles that are replicas of the museum's original collection. Centring the

display is Wawadiƚła, an authentic Kwakiutl family house built by Mungo Martin in 1953. Although it is not a public facility, the interior remains in use for ceremonial purposes and includes a dance screen, log drum, and a 1913 carving of Sisiutł, a dreaded two-headed serpent.

Looking at the many new and ancient poles, the question arises, what represents a "legitimate" totem? In 2017 a public school in Ontario was encouraged to remove a "totem" created by its students in the 1970s. The carving had been an effort by the students to educate themselves on the hardships faced by Indigenous Peoples following the European invasion of the seventeenth century. Its removal followed a complaint from, and subsequent consultations with, nearby First Nations Peoples, who deemed the pole an affront to their cultural beliefs and therefore culturally inappropriate.

While most First Nations Peoples rely on oral tradition to preserve their stories, the totem pole remains a visual link to the history and legacy of West Coast Indigenous cultures.

FOURTEEN

HEAD-SMASHED-IN BUFFALO JUMP

From a distance, the limestone escarpment that rises above the rolling prairie eighteen kilometres northwest of Fort Macleod, Alberta, looks like nothing out of the ordinary, but on closer inspection it represents the location of the largest and best-preserved buffalo jump in North America.

While human habitation of the area dates back more than 9,000 years, the buffalo jumps did not see use until around 5,700 years ago, although artifacts gathered at the Alberta site suggest that this site was more in use only during the last 1,800 years.

The name may sound unusual, but a buffalo jump is pretty much as the name suggests: a cliff over which herds of buffalo plunged to their demise.

For the various prairie-dwelling Niisitapi, the buffalo was their lifeblood. The massive mammals provided them with food, fuel, clothing, and tools, and had been doing so for thousands of years. So it was crucial to devise an efficient way to harvest the number of beasts needed to last a year.

Each autumn, the Niisitapi would follow the buffalo to their fall pastures in the Porcupine Hills of southwestern Alberta. Each hunt would begin with a ritual ceremony, after which the buffalo runners would head out to locate the herds. With their extensive knowledge of buffalo behaviour, the runners would disguise themselves in animal hides and lure the buffalo forward to the ten-metre-high cliffs. They did this by getting ahead of the herd and imitating the bleating of a lost calf.

Then the buffalo hunters would herd the animals into a narrowing V-shaped enclosure that consisted of rows of stone cairns and ended at the lip of the high cliff. As the herd moved toward the sound, large numbers of the Niisitapi would race up from behind the cairns and scare the herd into a moving, unstoppable mass hurtling toward their doom.

Once below the cliff, the hunters would butcher the beasts and boil the parts in large cauldrons, drying others on racks to provide a winter's supply of pemmican. Horns were scraped to create spoons, while the tongues were given to the medicine men and women to assure the success of the hunts.

Not surprisingly, much feasting and dancing accompanied the successful hunt.

But the circle of life was not to last. The use of the rifle ended the need for the buffalo jumps. In the 1870s the European invaders who had taken over the lands in eastern Canada wanted more. A railway was being planned to bring the western

The cliff over which the Niisitapi drove the buffalo they hunted can be seen clearly in this photo from the Head-Smashed-In Buffalo Jump Interpretation Centre.

territories into the newly created Dominion of Canada. In 1877, to make way for the tracks, a treaty forced the Niisitapi onto dusty reserves, while the buffalo herds were decimated by eastern hunters. Meanwhile, the Niisitapi were decimated by starvation and smallpox. The buffalo hunting died, and the jumps were forgotten.

Then, in 1938, James Bird of the American Museum of Natural History uncovered a massive mound of buffalo bones beneath a cliff in

As European settlers moved westward, they eradicated the millions of buffalo, shipping off their bones by rail to be used as fertilizer.

southwestern Alberta. The find consisted of some hundred thousand animals. Smaller mounds were unearthed nearby. Bird had uncovered the remains of a buffalo jump, a term unknown to most Canadians.

In 1981 UNESCO designated the site a World Heritage Site for its "remarkable testimony of prehistoric life bearing witness to customs practised for 6,000 years" and ranked it with the pyramids of Egypt and the Galapagos Islands for its significance.

To commemorate this First Nations heritage and to preserve the site, Parks Canada opened an interpretation centre in 1987 a short distance from the buffalo jump. Designed by Robert LeBlond, the $9.8 million structure (for which he later won the prestigious Governor General's Award for Architecture) consists of five levels that recount the life of the Niisitapi and the story of the hunt itself, while the exterior is designed to blend with the adjacent cliffs.

Tours start with the top level and views of the surrounding lands where the great herds once roamed. Here, too, are some of the surviving stone cairns that funneled the animals to the clifftops. Visitors then move down to the first and second levels to understand the world that the people lived in and have a glimpse into their lifestyles.

Re-creations of the buffalo poised to leap from the cliff form the third level of the display.

Lower levels indicate the methods that archaeologists have used to research this and other sites. Exit is through the gift shop.

Alberta does have many other prehistoric Indigenous sites. Writing-on-Stone Provincial Park reveals pictographs dating back more than 1,700 years. The Majorville Cairn and Medicine Wheel site represents an ancient Niisitapi ritual centre that dates back more than 4,500 years and continues to be used today. The site consists of a nine-metre-wide central cairn connected by twenty-eight spokes to a surrounding twenty-seven-metre-wide stone circle.

The Bodo Bison Skulls archaeological site is, at seven square kilometres, the largest archaeological site in Canada and consists of thousands of buffalo skulls, along with campsites and artifacts. Visitors may participate in the ongoing digs.

Near Lethbridge, the Fincastle bison kill site, uncovered in 2015 and dating back 2,500 years, reveals more than two hundred thousand buffalo bones. A feature that continues to puzzle the researchers is that several of the animal bones were placed in an upright position for no apparent reason.

The name "Head-Smashed-In" does not refer to the death throes of the animals. Niisitapi oral tradition says that the name comes from the fate of a young Niisitapi boy who wanted to watch the jump from a position below the cliff, a decision that proved to be deadly.

FIFTEEN

THE TIDE IS HIGH:
FUNDY'S GIANT TIDES

FUNDY'S WORLD-FAMOUS TIDES

This song title by the rock group Blondie was not referring to the world's highest tides, those which surge up the Bay of Fundy between New Brunswick and Nova Scotia twice daily. Yet, these watery phenomena have gained as much if not more world attention and attract tens of thousands of visitors to these shores every year.

Rising to the height of a four-storey building, these ocean surges are the result of the Bay of Fundy's unusual shape and length. While tides are normal around the world, those in Fundy are explained by Parks Canada this way: "[As in a basin], water will slosh back and forth in response to a disturbance such as wind [a phenomenon noted in Ontario's Lake Erie] … or a tidal push. Because of the particular length of the Bay of Fundy [150 kilometres], the timing or period of that sloshing coincides with the tidal push from the Atlantic…. These two movements resonate and amplify one another to create the giant tides."

The surge begins as little more than a ripple extending across the mouth of the bay; it quickly picks up speed and height as the shores of the bay narrow, until at the narrow head of the bay, the tides reach up to sixteen metres high.

But it doesn't stop there. Feeding into the head of the bay are the waters of the Petitcodiac, Salmon, and Hebert Rivers. As the incoming tidal surge meets the outflow from the rivers, it crests into a speeding wave that reaches three metres high. Known as tidal bores, they are found in many rivers around the globe where the incoming tides clash with outflowing rivers. The Amazon River in Brazil boasts a tidal bore that looms four metres high, rushes in at twenty kilometres per hour, and has become popular with surfers. But that on the Qiantang River in China, at nine metres high and reaching speeds of forty kilometres per hour, the world's highest, would not only intimidate such recreation but often damages riverside vessels and shops as it roars upstream. Moncton's River Walk allows curious onlookers opportunities to easily view this natural phenomenon.

Then, six hours later, all becomes quiet. The flow of the river returns to normal, while in the bay, the receding waters expose vast mud flats with their many plants and sea creatures.

Many locations along the shores of the Bay of Fundy offer curious visitors opportunities to experience this world-renowned phenomenon. Perhaps the most stunning location is the Hopewell Rocks Provincial Park located south of Moncton along Highway NB 114. These flowerpot-shaped pillars have resulted from thousands of years of erosion, most of which is due to the swirling tides. The soft layers of red sandstone, created in turn by the erosion of an ancient mountain range, that underlie a hard cap of conglomerate have washed away, resulting in a forest of pillars of many unusual shapes that loom above the shining mud flats. Names like Mother-in-Law Rock, Elephant Rock (the trunk recently collapsed), Turtle Rock, and Bear Rock reflect the shapes and forms of this seascape. In dramatic contrast, the high tides virtually cover the pillars entirely.

With the tide out and the shining mud flats open, visitors clamber down the cliffs to walk the 2.5 kilometres of open ocean floor. Here, they may observe a variety of plant and animal life found only on the seabed, including barnacles, periwinkles, limpets, and crabs, along with mud shrimp, sea anemones, and rare forms of jellyfish.

Highway NB 114 then continues to wind along the coast to the fishing village of Alma. Here, at the mouth of the Upper Salmon River, Mi'kmaq people canoed along the coast and up the river, gathering a catch of salmon and other fish. By the early 1800s, squatters began to show up and established a crude settlement known as Upper Salmon River. The influx of Irish immigrants in the 1840s enlarged the community, while industries like sawmilling and ship building began to create an economic base for the fledgling village, which soon changed its name to Alma.

By the end of the nineteenth century, the depletion of the forests ended logging and the other industries as well. That left only the fishers to troll the waters for lobster and scallops. That remained the community's economic mainstay until 1948, when the federal government's Parks Department realized that some sort of impetus was needed in the Maritimes and created the Fundy National Park. Today Alma has become the park's headquarters and is noted as well for its seafood delicacies and festivals.

Here, too, is one of the more dramatic images of the tidal phenomenon: the dozen or so fishing boats that bob by the wharf at high tide lie on the mud flats nearly fifteen metres below when the waters have vanished.

The fishing boats of the port of Alma, New Brunswick, in the Bay of Fundy are stranded when the tide is out.

At 206 square kilometres, the park extends from Alma to beyond Point Wolfe on the coast and inland as far as Shepody Road. The park includes campgrounds and one hundred kilometres of trails that lead along the shore and to waterfalls and historic sites, such as the Wolfe Point covered bridge. Park staff offer beach walks to teach visitors about the many forms of life that the extreme tides expose.

In 2011 the Royal Astronomical Society of Canada certified Fundy National Park as Canada's thirteenth "dark sky" reserve. The dark sky initiative began in 1999 with the certification of the Torrance Barrens near Gravenhurst, Ontario, and has gone on to include Point Pelee National Park, Jasper National Park, and Bruce Peninsula National Park, among the seventeen such designations up to the present. Within such designated areas, the number, design, and location of artificial lighting is strictly controlled to reduce any light pollution that would interfere with the views of the stunning stellar displays in the night skies.

At the west end of the park, the Fundy Trail Parkway is found. Access to this scenic drive, however, is farther west and begins about ten kilometres east of the coastal village of St. Martins. For nineteen kilometres, this paved route winds along the shore and veers around steep switchback curves, offering nearly two dozen lookouts across the bay. The Parkway Interpretive Centre is located at Big Salmon River, the head for several trails that lead to waterfalls, forests, and to the Hearst Lodge.

This simple log building was built by William Randolph Hearst as his private fishing lodge (one of many built by prominent Americans) and now offers meals and limited accommodation to those who are undaunted by hiking a challenging 2.7-kilometre forested trail from the interpretive centre. For others, a pickup truck or ATV will lumber off through the woods to the riverside retreat. Anyone wanting a break from the connected outside world will be pleased to find the lodge free of TVs and internet hookups. A wide porch overlooks the rushing river, while a small dining room serves up meals in front of a stone fireplace.

In 2007 a pair of local groups including the Bay of Fundy Ecosystem Group and the Bay of Fundy Product Club succeeded in lobbying UNESCO to designate a 430,000-hectare area as a World Biosphere Reserve. As with other such locations, the reserve incorporates a core area of twenty thousand hectares, which is based on the national park, and is enclosed by a buffer area and zone of transition. The overall designation extends from St. Martins to the Tantramar Marshes and inland as far as Moncton.

The Hopewell Rocks, Alma, and Fundy National Park lie along Highway NB 114 south of either Moncton, a distance of 79 kilometres, or from Sussex, a distance of 60.5 kilometres, both of which are situated on the Trans-Canada Highway east of Saint John. St. Martins and the Fundy Trail Parkway can be reached along Highway NB 111, 54 kilometres east from Saint John.

FACING: The famous Hopewell Rocks, Bay of Fundy.

SIXTEEN

IN THE FOOTSTEPS OF THE VIKINGS:
FOLLOWING NEWFOUNDLAND'S VIKING TRAIL

THE VIKINGS

Western Newfoundland's Highway 430 did not earn its designation as the Viking Trail because the ancient Vikings followed that route. Rather, it leads to the vestiges of North America's only authenticated Norse settlement. In 1975 the National Historic Sites and Monuments Board of Canada declared L'Anse aux Meadows as a National Historic Site.

One of UNESCO's first World Heritage Sites, L'Anse aux Meadows was inscribed in 1978 and contains nine excavated eleventh-century structures. Adjacent to the excavations, Parks Canada has re-created the Viking encampment, offering visitors a chance to delve into the life of these adventurers as told by costumed interpreters.

They start by clearing up what a "Viking" is. The term does not refer to a place of origin but rather meant "raiders," usually hailing from the Scandinavian region of Europe. In fact, the term itself was not coined until the nineteenth century.

Vikings were noted for their fearless forays into the British Isles and western Europe beginning around the tenth century, a scourge that lasted for at least two hundred years. That sense of adventure led them to seek new lands and to sail west and settle Iceland and later Greenland.

The Greenlanders Sagas, recorded in Iceland toward the end of the fourteenth century by an unknown writer, describe the accidental discovery of previously unknown territory located south and west of Greenland. They recount how a merchant named Bjarni Herjólfsson was blown by a vicious storm beyond Greenland and on to an unknown landfall somewhere in North America. From there he returned to Greenland carrying supplies of wood and grapes, and so was born the search for Vinland, for wood was scarce in Greenland and grapes an unheard-of luxury.

Soon after, one Thorfinn Karlsefni set sail for this mythical land with an estimated 250 prospective colonizers. They landed near the northern tip of the Great North Peninsula of northwestern Newfoundland. Here, on a promising meadow beside Black Duck Brook, the group established what is most likely North America's first European settlement, nearly five centuries before Christopher Columbus made landfall in the West Indies.

However, their relations with the area's inhabitants (which the Vikings called skraelings) proved troublesome, and after an estimated three years, the group packed up and retreated to Greenland. After that the meadows took over again, and the site was subsequently occupied by the local Indigenous population.

Then in 1960, seeking to verify the existence of the elusive Vinland, Helge Ingstad, a Norwegian author and explorer, and his wife, Anne, were led to some strange mounds beside a brook in northwestern Newfoundland, a location that locals had simply called the "Indian camp."

After eight years of research, the Ingstads concluded that, while this may not have been Vinland, it was clearly a thousand-year-old Viking encampment. In 1975 the Canadian National Historic Sites and Monuments Board declared the finding a National Historic Site. Three years later UNESCO listed it as a World Heritage Site for being "the first and only known site by the Vikings in North America … and a unique milestone in the history of human migration and discovery."

Carbon dating put the habitation at between 990 and 1050 CE, with a likely population of up to 160 inhabitants. The largest structure so far excavated measures 28.8 metres by 15.6 metres and was a sod over wooden frame habitation and showed evidence of having several rooms. Other structures were an iron smithy, a carpentry workshop, and a boat repair shop. Thanks to this discovery, other possible Norse sites are currently being explored.

Today Parks Canada administers the site. The visitor centre and museum display many of the artifacts uncovered during excavation, including bone needles, a bronze pin, and a stone oil lamp. A walkway leads to the excavation site itself and to three re-created Viking structures where some of the typical Viking crafts are re-enacted. Here, too, visitors hear stories of early Norse exploits, all capably narrated by costumed re-enactors.

The Trail

The only route to this ancient site is along the Viking Trail. A signed highway beginning on the Trans-Canada Highway 1 at Deer Falls, Newfoundland, it starts off with still another UNESCO World Heritage Site, Gros Morne National Park, created in 1973. At 1,805 square kilometres, it represents the third-largest national park in eastern Canada. The UN body says "the fjords, waterfalls and geological structures combine to produce a landscape of high scenic value." It became a World Heritage Site in 1987.

Gros Morne lies along the Viking Trail thirty-nine kilometres from Deer Lake. Not only does it have Newfoundland's highest mountain at 806 metres, but it also displays the unusual rock known as peridotite, usually found well below the earth's surface but here thrust upward through the massive collision of two tectonic plates. The lack of nutrients in this parent rock has produced a desert-like barren surface. Unlike the jagged peaks usually associated with mountains, the mountains here form a tableland plateau separated by an inlet, Bonne Bay. As Highway 430 skirts the scenic north shore of Bonne Bay, the tableland massif soars high above the opposite shore of the bay.

The stunning mountains and rare geology of Gros Morne National Park, a World Heritage Site, attract thousands of visitors to Newfoundland's Northern Peninsula.

The park's discovery centre is located along Highway 431 on the south side of the bay, while the park entrance lies on the north side on Highway 430, seventy kilometres from Deer Lake. A ferry service connects the two shores.

Stunning trails lead from the discovery centre to the heights of the tablelands, while another trail leads from the visitor centre to the top of Gros Morne Mountain.

The park's most iconic image, however, lies farther along the coast, and that is the lake known as West Brook Pond (lakes in Newfoundland are known as "ponds"), which, at thirty kilometres, is the world's longest and deepest freshwater fjord. Here, the vertical cliffs plunge from 350 metres into the clear lake waters, creating a vista that nearly every Newfoundland and Labrador travel ad prominently features. From those heights, Pissing Mare Falls plunges into the water below, making it the highest waterfall in eastern North America. (Its curious name is likely responsible for its being relatively unpublicized.)

To reach the fjord, a trail leads from the parking lot on the highway to the shore, where boat tours are offered. So popular has the excursion become that reservations should be made ahead of time. Steep, lengthy trails lead to the summits of the cliffs themselves.

From the park, the Viking Trail continues for 340 kilometres along Highway 430, passing through a string of fishing villages, some of which are now little more than a few homes along the road. Others, such as St. Paul's, offer restaurants and accommodation as well as a theatre.

As the mountains fade into the background, the terrain along the coast becomes flatter, dotted with numerous ponds.

Port Saunders, 104 kilometres from the park, has grown into a busy lobster fishing centre, with numerous lobster boats bobbing at wharf side awaiting the short-lived annual lobster season to harvest the clawed delicacy.

St. Barbe, eighty-three kilometres farther along, is a key centre from which ferry service connects Newfoundland with Blanc-Sablon in Quebec across the Strait of Belle Isle. The MV *Apollo* requires about one hour and forty-five minutes to complete the crossing, which it performs two or three times daily.

Passing through Eddies Cove, the trail swings inland for 123 kilometres to reach the opposite side of the Great North Peninsula at St. Anthony, a location first identified by Jacques Cartier in 1534 as a haven for Basque fishing fleets.

It is from this last stretch that Highway 436 branches off to the L'Anse aux Meadows site.

St. Anthony is the largest community north of Deer Lake. With its population of 2,500, it offers a range of accommodation, restaurants (including the usual fast-food chains), and social services, such as schools, banks, and stores.

If the visitor wants more Viking experiences, the village of Norstead, about two kilometres north of the Parks Canada site, has re-created a Viking port of trade with replica structures that include a Viking sailing vessel. It was established in 2000 as a nonprofit operation to celebrate the thousandth anniversary of the Viking arrival. Here, too, one will find the appropriately named Viking Village, Valhalla Bed and Breakfast, and the Norseman Restaurant.

Unfortunately, the Viking Trail is not a circle route, so the return trip is back the same way.

Two other UNESCO sites in Newfoundland and Nova Scotia also reflect Canada's earliest settlement challenges.

RED BAY

Some five centuries after the Vikings came and went, Basque fishermen began to show up. In the mid-sixteenth century, they established one of their many

Newfoundland's Viking Trail leads to the site of a tenth-century Viking settlement, which is now restored by Parks Canada and is a designated World Heritage Site.

whaling stations at Gran Baya on the Labrador coast. They crossed the ocean, coming from France and Spain to hunt the bowhead and right whales, rendering their blubber into oil, which was processed on shore. The location, now known as Red Bay, was the largest of the Basque whaling stations.

Events in Europe led the English to close the strait to the Basques, who vacated the sites. Saddle Island, a short boat ride from shore, contains the ruins of the tryworks and a cemetery that is the final resting place of the 130 men who perished here during their short stay. Two interpretation centres administered by Parks Canada recount the stories of the fishers' lives, and one displays a restored chalupa, the type of whaling boat that the whalers used to locate and harpoon the whales. It has been a National Historic Site since 1979 and a UNESCO World Heritage Site since 2013.

Grand Pré, Nova Scotia

The Grand Pré, Nova Scotia, UNESCO World Heritage Site, also a National Historic Site of Canada, is a rare example of seventeenth-century marshland recovery in Canada. Around 1680, Acadian settlers moved from Port Royal to the marshlands of the Minas Basin, called the "Grand Pré" (great meadow), where they created a French-style diking system to drain and desalinate a thousand hectares of marsh in order to establish their farms. By the 1740s a line of 150 dwellings lined the dikes, making the settlement the most populated of the area's three Acadian districts.

After the British gained control of the area in 1755, they demanded that the Acadians swear loyalty to the Crown or otherwise face deportation. The proud Acadians refused to do so, and by 1762 a population of more than 6,000, including 2,200 from Grand Pré, had been exiled to such locations as Louisiana, a tragic event called "Le Grand Dérangement."

Those who did return found their homes in the hands of the British occupiers. It remains an emotional focus for Acadians to this day, and even now Grand Pré remains the cultural heartland of Nova Scotia's Acadian community.

A memorial church, a visitor centre, and a statue of Evangeline, the heroine of Henry Wadsworth Longfellow's 1847 poem "Evangeline, a Tale of Acadie," pay tribute to that legacy. The statue was commissioned by the Canadian Pacific Railway, which owned the rail line through the area, to attract tourism. The ridge-top visitor centre offers views across the drained marshlands to the water of the Minas Basin. The site lies adjacent to the town of Wolfville, Nova Scotia, about eighty kilometres west of Halifax. It became a National Historic Site in 1982 and a UNESCO World Heritage Site in 2012.

SEVENTEEN

WELCOME TO CANADA:
FROM GROSSE-ÎLE TO PIER 21

Canada is highly regarded around the world for its diversity and, in recent years, for welcoming large numbers of refugees fleeing persecution in Syria. Today Canada can boast of having some of the most welcoming and diverse cities in the world.

Canada's early years, however, were not so enlightened. In fact, one of the first acts by Europeans in Canada was when Étienne Brûlé planted a flag on the shores of the Baie-des-Chaleurs on the Gaspé Peninsula in 1584 and claimed the territory for France, basically ignoring the fact that the place already belonged to someone else, namely First Nations Peoples.

The First Nations felt that the land and its natural resources were for all to share. The European invaders, however, didn't see it that way. They believed in private or government ownership, and the Indigenous inhabitants were not part of their world.

As private seigneuries swallowed up land along the St. Lawrence and the shores of the Great Lakes, dubious treaties corralled Indigenous Peoples and shipped them off to reserves — and not always willingly.

Even in more modern times, mistreatment continued. Beginning in the late 1800s, the federal government and Canada's churches felt that Indigenous children needed to be stripped of their "savage" ways and become "Canadianized." This led to the creation of residential schools. Under this policy, authorities rounded up the children and placed them in schools run primarily by the major churches, far from their home, their language, and their culture.

Over the years, more than 150,000 children were removed from their families. The teachers basically stripped them of their culture and their language, subjecting them to unduly harsh punishments (such as simply for speaking their own language) and, in some instances, to sexual abuse.

As awareness grew over the damaging cultural and emotional impacts of the schools, the churches and the government gradually closed them down, the last only in 1996. Over the following years, the churches and the government offered apologies, even as recently as 2017, while awarding financial compensations to the many victims, but much of the damage had already been done.

First Nations Peoples were not the only victims of forced removals. These date back to the 1750s. Following their victory over the French in Canada, the British deported large populations of Acadians for refusing to swear allegiance to the British Crown. Many were later allowed back in only to find their lands and properties no longer theirs.

Canada's doors, however, were open to some. Refugees fleeing war and persecution in the United States following the American Revolution, beginning in 1784, were given land in Canada and the Maritimes and were known as United Empire Loyalists. Irish immigration began in earnest in the 1820s, settling in places like the Ottawa Valley and the Peterborough region. Poles arrived to take up land in the Ottawa Valley in the 1850s. Pretty soon Canada had become a mosaic of primarily European settlements.

GROSSE-ÎLE

In the 1820s the dramatic influx of Irish immigrants brought with it outbreaks of cholera. To reduce that danger, the British government established a quarantine station on Grosse-Île in the St. Lawrence River, forty-eight kilometres downstream from Quebec City, the main destination for these arrivals. All immigrant ships were required to dock here while the passengers were vetted for cholera. Those who were ill were quarantined, while their healthy relatives were quartered in hotels built for that purpose. Once cleared, the ships continued to Quebec City.

Cholera, which had spread from India to Europe, led to further outbreaks in 1834, 1849, and 1854. The great potato famine in Ireland, exacerbated by ruthless landlords, brought more waves of Irish streaming into Canada in 1847, many carrying typhus. In fact, one landlord alone, one Denis Mahon, had evicted more than 1,450 impoverished tenants from his lands in Roscommon County.

The island facilities, however, were no match for the thousands of sick and starving Irish, having a mere two hundred beds for the twelve thousand being held on the island. Sick and healthy were forced to share tents, which exacerbated the spread of the disease.

Thousands of ill Irish died even while en route on what were often labelled "coffin ships." More than 4,900 died at sea before they even arrived. So severe was the crisis that ships often anchored for days in the river, waiting their turn to dock, leading to still more deaths. With five thousand burials in the island's cemetery, Grosse-Île today contains the largest Great Famine burial ground outside of Ireland.

Following Confederation in 1867, the new government of Canada named Dr. Frederick Montizambert as the director of the facility. He immediately embarked on a series of changes, replacing the many dilapidated structures and dividing the island into three sections: the eastern section held the sick, the western section housed the healthy, and the middle section contained a small village for the island's staff. He also streamlined the inspection process and ordered the construction of a new hospital. In 1909 a Celtic cross fifteen metres high was erected on the west end of the island to commemorate the many deaths.

The island remained a quarantine station until 1932, after which most new immigrants had begun to arrive at Pier 21 in Halifax.

The Memorial Cross in Grosse-Île was erected in memory of the many, predominantly Irish, immigrants who died there following harrowing voyages in disease-ridden ships.

During the Second World War, Grosse-Île became part of the military operations, after which it passed to the Department of Agriculture.

Recognizing the significance of Grosse-Île for its role in Canada's immigration challenges, and the horrendous conditions that the thousands of Irish migrants faced, in 1974 the National Historic Sites and Monuments Board designated Grosse-Île and the Irish Memorial as a National Historic Site. Following that designation, visitors began to arrive. Over the years, many pilgrimages took place to the cemetery and the cross and the grounds where so many Irish now rest.

Today's visitors are anxious to understand the hardships of the times, and the many surviving structures help them to relive that tragic era. Ferry service brings them to the island, where the former hotels stand close to the dock. The hotels were segregated into three separate buildings — three classes to reflect the classes of passengers on the ships. Closest to the wharf, the first-class hotel offered the most amenities, while the third-class hotel lacked even washstands in the rooms — its walls did not even extend to the ceiling. The second-class hotel, erected in 1893, was originally the first-class accommodation until the new hotel opened in 1912. The current third-class hotel was completed in 1914.

Visitors today may choose between a guided tour and a self-guided tour. Trams are available to conduct the visitors along the road connecting the three sectors.

Today's arrivals, as did those early Irish arrivals, must undergo an "inspection" in the old disinfection station at the dock. Uniformed "nurses" insist throats and temperatures are checked before allowing anyone to proceed.

From the dock and the hotels, the route leads past an 1893 guardhouse, a bakery, and the Anglican chapel, which was built in 1877 and rests on a high rock outcrop. Farther along, the trail leads to the site of the island's former staff village, named Saint-Luc-du-Grosse-Île. Most of that housing has gone, but the Catholic chapel built in 1874 remains, as does a school.

The eastern hospital sector contains the former homes of the doctor and bacteriologist, the 1912 nurses' residence, and the 1908 hospital superintendent's home. The island's oldest structure, and the only original quarantine building to remain, is the lazaretto, or hospital, built in 1847 and now furnished as its patients would have seen it.

Most visitors will pay tribute to the unfortunate Irish at the Celtic Cross and at the granite memorial erected in 1998, which lists the names of those deceased and those who strove to care for them. In all, some thirty-five historic structures are to be found on the island.

Visitors may wish to follow the nature trails that lead through the natural areas of the island and to a lookout over the river. There is no overnighting, but refreshments are available in the former third-class hotel.

Canada did not always welcome immigrants. While some black people were permitted into Canada because of their service in the British military during the American Revolution and the War of 1812, or via the Underground Railroad, a law passed in 1911 barred black people from entering Canada on the basis that they were not suited to the climate, a law that remained on the books until 1962.

In 1914 the passenger ship the *Komagata Maru* arrived off the coast of Vancouver and was promptly halted by a British gunboat. Many of the 374 Punjabi Sikhs on board were fleeing persecution in India and sought refugee status. The government considered them agitators and sent them home. While twenty-four were admitted to the country, all the remaining Sikhs, Hindus, and Muslims were barred.

The infamous Chinese head tax placed on arriving Chinese men, most of whom were put to work building the CPR, was imposed in 1885 and raised in 1904, effectively preventing Chinese men in Canada from bringing their relatives. In 1924 Chinese immigration was stopped altogether, a restriction that lasted until 1947.

But the most damning of all was the tragedy of the MS *St. Louis.*

In 1939 Captain Gustav Schröder was desperately seeking refuge for his more than nine hundred mostly Jewish passengers, who were escaping the pogroms of Nazi Germany. After first failing to find safe haven in either Cuba or the United States, they arrived at Halifax, where they were turned back, with the Canadian government shamefully proclaiming of the Jewish refugees that "one is too many." While some were eventually accepted by Britain, many ended up in France, Belgium, and the Netherlands, all of which fell under Nazi control.

PIER 21

By the time the operations at Grosse-Île were winding down, Pier 21 in Halifax had begun welcoming arriving immigrants. In fact, as early as 1880, Halifax had been processing immigrants arriving on the newly inaugurated ocean liners that could not be accommodated at Grosse-Île.

Within a few decades, it had become clear that the original facility was being overwhelmed by the size of the ships and numbers of passengers. Because of the great Halifax explosion of 1917, any attempt to construct a new facility had to be delayed. Finally, in 1928 a new terminal complex opened at the south end of the city and included grain terminals, a new hotel, a train station, and an immigration shed known as Pier 21.

After the immigrants completed their processing and medicals in the new shed, an overhead walkway led them to the customs clearing shed area as well as the tracks, where the Canadian National Railway (CNR) trains would carry the new arrivals toward their final destinations. They were usually crowded onto badly outdated colonist cars with wooden seats and stoves for cooking. Hardly a warm welcome. (In contrast, regular train passengers boarded comfortable, modern coaches at the new CN station.)

The earliest arrivals were largely from Britain and the Netherlands, while those from southern and eastern Europe were largely discouraged before they could even depart, or, as in the case of the *St. Louis*, they were barred entirely. Despite a drop in immigration during the Depression, the terminal welcomed the new cruise ship era with visitors disembarking for brief visits to the historic port city.

But all this came to a crashing halt with the outbreak of war.

The terminal was quickly transformed into a port of embarkation for troop ships and their escort vessels bound for Europe. During this difficult period, arrivals usually consisted of wounded soldiers, children, and a few important visitors, such as Winston Churchill and Princess Juliana and Prince Bernhard of the Netherlands. For this and for helping to liberate the Netherlands in the war, Canada receives a yearly gift of tulips from that grateful country.

Not too surprisingly, the postwar years witnessed a new surge in immigrants, including displaced persons from war-torn Europe, British war brides and their children, and Jewish refugees. (Authorities, it seems, had awakened to the horrors of the Holocaust.) The 1950s saw Italian workers streaming in to new jobs and Hungarian refugees fleeing the Soviet invasion of their homeland in 1956.

Still, Canada's immigration policies and their implementation remained highly discriminatory. Persons of colour and those from eastern Europe were still being discouraged or even turned away completely. This ended with a new Immigration Act in 1953, while discrimination by race did not officially end until 1963.

Then, with the increase of international air travel, the need for Pier 21 waned. Following the arrival of the last ship, the SS *Nieuw Amsterdam*, in 1971, the facility was closed.

For the following twenty years, Pier 21 housed a naval school. Now, in addition to providing space for various arts groups, Pier 21 is a popular stop for cruise ships, and the adjacent terminals, Piers 20 and 22, became reception centres and gift shops for the ships' passengers.

In 1997 the Historic Sites and Monuments Board of Canada declared Pier 21 a National Historic Site and two years later opened the Canadian Museum of Immigration at Pier 21. Across the lane, an artists' collective and craft brewery moved into the Pier 21 annex.

Today visitors arrive to learn the evolution of the Pier 21 immigration story as well as personal and first-hand accounts of the experiences of immigrants arriving to a strange new land. Beyond the exhibits, Pier 21 also houses a vast collection of archival images, documents, and first-hand accounts from new arrivals. The collection also goes into the challenges presented by Canada's often discriminatory policies and delves into First Nations history and the arrivals of the earliest Europeans.

In 2015 a memorial to the MS *St. Louis* was placed in the lobby to highlight the rampant anti-Semitism that led to the Mackenzie government denying entry to the more than nine hundred Jewish refugees arriving on that fateful ship in 1939.

Immigration to Canada has not always been welcomed (it still isn't in some regions of the country), but Pier 21 offers a special opportunity for museum visitors to witness the joys and disappointments of new arrivals who were trying to make Canada their new home.

RMS *Majestic* alongside the Nova Scotian Hotel in 1934. Pier 20 is on the left, and Pier 21 is on the right.

TORONTO, THE DIVER-CITY

Toronto has come a long way since the days when more than 80 percent of its residents were British-born and the annual Orange Parade marked the domination by the city's Protestants. Decades later, in 2016, with more than 51 percent of the city being foreign-born, Toronto has become the world's most diverse city, according to the BBC — a far cry from the times when the immigration policy was white people only and when Jewish people were excluded from public parks.

In fact, the city can count more than 250 different ethnic groups. Many of them enjoy their own neighbourhoods and shopping districts: Little Italy, Little Jamaica, Gerrard Indian Bazaar, Greektown, and six Chinatowns. Today Chinese Canadians make

BAPS Shri Swaminarayan Mandir is a Hindu temple built in Toronto, Ontario. Completed in July 2007 after only eighteen months of construction, the temple is made up of twenty-four thousand hand-carved pieces of Italian Carrara marble, Turkish limestone, and Indian pink stone.

up more than 90 percent of the population in certain sections of northeast Toronto, where they shop at North America's largest Chinese mall, the Pacific Mall. To the west, in neighbouring Brampton, South Asians constitute 80 percent of the population and boast grand Sikh and Hindu temples.

Toronto's immigrant population is responsible for some of the city's newest and most stunning architectural landmarks. In 2014 the Aga Khan Museum opened in Toronto. This ten-thousand-square-metre building is considered unique in the world and houses Islamic art and displays of Islamic contributions to history, science, and culture. The museum is dedicated to the preservation and display of cultural and religious traditions of diverse Muslim communities. An elaborate park surrounds the structure.

The BAPS Shri Swaminarayan Mandir (temple), with its delicate white spires rising above the industrial wasteland of north Etobicoke, comes as a surprise to drivers travelling the 427 north of Highway 401. To create this masterpiece, specialized carvers spent eighteen months hand-carving twenty-four thousand pieces of Italian marble, Turkish limestone, and Indian pink stone, all in accordance with ancient Hindu practices. The remarkable structure contains neither nails nor mortar. The holy building was consecrated in July 2007 and is the largest such temple in Canada.

Today most cities across the country can boast mosques, synagogues, and temples, and even Arctic towns like Iqaluit and Inuvik, with its "little mosque on the tundra," claim mosques of their own. Clearly, Canada has earned its reputation of welcoming immigrants and refugees fleeing persecution. Only now they need no longer fear that "one is too many."

EIGHTEEN

BEHIND THOSE WALLS:
OLD QUEBEC CITY WORLD HERITAGE SITE

The sight of a horse-drawn carriage clopping through a stone gate is an image of another era, reminiscent of medieval Europe. And in a way that is what Old Quebec is. Founded by explorer Samuel de Champlain in 1608, this historic wonder has been described by UNESCO as "one of the best examples of a fortified colonial city … unique north of Mexico," a description that earned the city its inscription as a UNESCO World Heritage Site in 1985, one of that organization's earliest designations in Canada.

Within that designation, the city consists of an upper and lower town. The oldest section is grouped around Place Royale close to the harbour, the site of Champlain's habitation. The newer town lies atop the cliffs within the historic walls that surround it.

Its defensible location high atop Cap Diamant was key to the early First Nations Peoples, who called it Stadacona. By 1690 the French, too, had recognized this and fortified the site with sturdy redoubts connected by a wooden palisade from which the local garrison successfully repelled a British attack in 1745.

It was only a few years after that when British general James Wolfe sent his troops to scale the steep cliffs in a pre-dawn raid where, on the Plains of Abraham, he defeated French general the Marquis de Montcalm in a skirmish that lasted only minutes. That was enough time, however, to claim the lives of both generals.

In 1819–21 the military victors replaced the older fortifications with sturdy stone ramparts, most of which stand today. That they survive is a credit to the heritage-minded then governor general Lord Dufferin, who resisted a proposal to demolish them in the late nineteenth century. The Fortifications of Quebec were originally designated as a National Historic Site in 1948 and became a UNESCO World Heritage Site in 1985.

Not all the history lies above the ground. In 2005–08 when work on the Dufferin Terrace, a walkway overlooking the river, was under way, workers discovered that beneath the walkway lay the remarkably well-preserved remains of one of the city's earliest chateaus, the Château Saint-Louis.

That first chateau was built by Governor Montmagny in 1647, replaced by Governor Frontenac in 1694, and later enlarged by Governor Vaudreuil. This final chateau was destroyed by fire in 1834 and largely forgotten as the Dufferin Terrace was built on top of it and the massive Château Frontenac beside it.

What the archeologists discovered were the remains of the entire basement of the last chateau, ruins that include latrines, hearths, ovens, a staircase, and portions of archways that connected the rooms. In 2010–11 Parks Canada undertook a restoration project and constructed an underground crypt around the old chateau's ruins to allow visitors to tour one of the city's ancient wonders.

The city's most prominent landmark, the lofty Château Frontenac, is by comparison a relative newcomer, having been built by the Canadian Pacific Railway in 1898 and expanded many times since. The railway's station, although outside the gated area, a splendid chateau-style construction, was added in 1915 and is considered one of North America's grandest urban train stations.

The Terrasse Dufferin extends for 426 metres along the top of the sixty-metre cliff, offering extensive

One of the narrow streets in the lower part of Old Quebec City, a UNESCO World Heritage Site.

views of the St. Lawrence River, where the narrows, which the Algonquin called "Kebec," gave birth to the present name.

The St. Louis Gate marks one of the gated entrances to the old city. Within those walls and gates lie stone buildings and narrow lanes, many of which date to the seventeenth and eighteenth centuries. Along Rue Saint-Louis, with its roadside string of ancient buildings, number 47 marks the house in which General Montcalm is said to have died after being wounded by the British on the Plains of Abraham. Number 34, which today houses a fine-dining restaurant, was built in 1674, one of the city's oldest houses, and displays the typical Quebec-style "ski slope" roof. (The curved slope allows the snow to slip off without blocking the doorway.)

Prominent among the other early structures are the Chapelle des Ursulines, built in 1642, and the Maison Jacquet from 1675. The tall, spired Vieux Séminaire dates to 1663; the inscription "SME" above its iron gate means "Séminaire des Missions Étrangères" (Seminary for Foreign Missions). The 1736 Maillou House now contains the tourist information office, behind which lies a well-preserved historic courtyard.

Lower Town Quebec represents a still older corner of the city and is the original townsite laid out beside the busy docks. The Côte de la Canoterie descends the steep hill through the Hope Gate (used to separate the inhabitants of Upper and Lower Town) to the narrow pedestrian streets below. Here, Place Royale is the original town square, dominated by the 1688 church Notre-Dame-des-Victoires. The Rue Saint-Paul houses the city's antique and boutique district, a pedestrian street lined with eighteenth- and nineteenth-century buildings. It is not, however, the city's narrowest street. That would be the Rue Sous-le-Cap a short distance away, once the home of the city's infamous red-light district. It measures a mere three metres wide.

The docks themselves have been modernized and house the ferry that crosses the river to the sister city of Lévis on the south shore.

The most prominent structure of the city, aside from the Château Frontenac, is the grand Citadel National Historic Site. It replaced the earlier forts sitting atop Cap Diamant and at thirty-seven hectares is the largest such structure in the country.

When the British stormed across the Plains of Abraham in 1759, the French military had been sheltered in only a crude half-finished fort, which the British quickly replaced. Fearful of further American invasions, between 1820 and 1831 the British enlarged it into a massive star-shaped stone bastion, much of which still stands. It remains the home base for the distinctively French-Canadian regiment formed in 1914, the Royal Twenty-Second Regiment or, more simply, the "Van Doos" (from the French, *vingt-deux*). Its highly regarded marching band is world famous.

Although still a military base, the grounds are open to the public to view the museum — Canada's second-largest military museum — or to watch the changing of the guard in the morning. During the ceremony, the visitor may meet the latest "Batisse,"

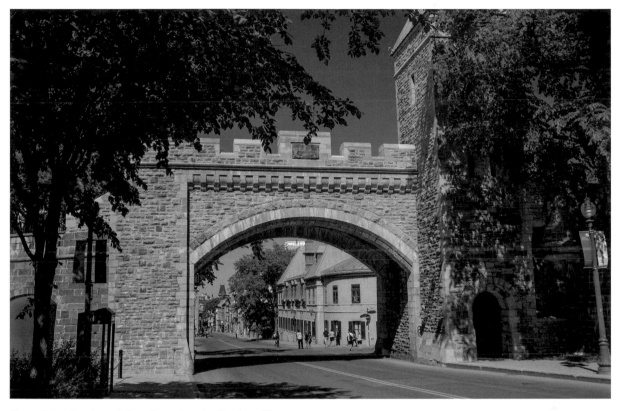

Porte Saint-Louis and Rue Saint-Louis, Quebec City.

the regiment's goat mascot, the first of which Queen Elizabeth presented to the Van Doos in 1955.

The grounds also contain a mausoleum dedicated to former governor general Georges Vanier, the Van Doos' first commander and Canada's first francophone governor general. The building houses the Books of Remembrance, which hold the names of all those in the regiment who died in combat. This building is not open to the public.

As a result of the heritage designations, and the city's own efforts to preserve its history through zoning and heritage regulations, Old Quebec attracts visitors by the busload from schools and from overseas as well as from within Canada. With its walls and early structures, it is one of the continent's historic wonders.

NINETEEN

BLUENOSE COUNTRY:
OLD TOWN LUNENBURG

Unique in North America, this authentic collection of eighteenth- and nineteenth-century wooden seaport structures is a UNESCO World Heritage Site and a National Historic Site of Canada. In addition, the town itself has further designated more than sixty individual buildings for heritage protection.

In 1753, when Britain had wrested control of North America from France, Nova Scotia's then governor, Edward Cornwallis, selected a site on a protected peninsula on Mahone Bay, southwest of Halifax, for a settlement of what he called "foreign Protestants." These were to be settlers of Germanic origin who he felt would be loyal to the British Crown and help hold in abeyance any influence from the French Catholics.

First he had to expel a group of Indigenous Mi'kmaq from their village of Mirligueche, which he did by simply burning their dwellings to the ground. And to further keep them at bay, he ordered a bounty on their scalps. (For this and other "accomplishments," the city of Halifax later erected a statue in his honour and named a park after him.)

This paved the way for noted British surveyor Charles Morris to lay out a grid network of streets on a hillside overlooking the harbour. A blockhouse closer to the end of the peninsula housed British troops to safeguard the vital settlement.

Lunenburg evolved into playing a vital role in the Maritime economy of Nova Scotia, shipping pine logs to the British navy for their ships' masts as well as salted cod to the West Indies in return for rum and molasses.

When the railways bypassed the community, and faster steam ships replaced the elegant schooners, the coastal trade routes moved away from the port. Still, the town continued to play a key role in the Atlantic fishery and especially in the building of schooners and wooden vessels.

Free from the damaging impacts of urban growth, the town has retained its early buildings and, happily, has also avoided devastating fires.

Lunenburg became famous as well for its production of one of the fastest schooners of the twentieth century: the *Bluenose*.

Designed by William J. Roue, a racing-boat specialist, the *Bluenose* was built in 1921 at the Smith and Rhuland Shipyard. Built as a fishing schooner, it was especially designed for speed to allow its crew to get their catch back to port first, to

The *Bluenose II*, a replica of the original *Bluenose*, lies in port.

get the highest prices. The *Bluenose* also participated in the International Fishermen's Race, in which it remained the world's fastest racing schooner for seventeen years. Nicknamed the Queen of the North Atlantic, it became the pride of the province and to this day decorates the back of the Canadian dime.

Its luck ran out, however, when it struck a reef and sank off the coast of Haiti in 1946.

In 1963 the same shipyard (and even some of the same craftsmen) launched the *Bluenose II*, a replica that has become a floating ambassador for the province and draws tourists to tour its decks or even to sign up as "crew for a day," where they participate in a working cruise on Mahone Bay.

As the tourist trade began to grow, the heritage of this distinctive collection of historic buildings was fast becoming recognized. In 1991 the federal government designated Old Town Lunenburg as a National Historic Site for its "numerous outstanding examples of vernacular architecture spanning more than 240 years."

In 1996, a submission to UNESCO brought Lunenburg esteemed recognition as a World Heritage Site, one of only two urban communities in North America to earn that status (the other being Old Town Quebec). UNESCO cited it as "an excellent example of a planned European settlement in North America, and the best surviving example of a British colonial town in North America."

In 1998 the town proceeded to honour its new-found status by designating Old Town Lunenburg as a heritage district, ensuring the preservation of its heritage structures and governing the appearance of

The port of Lunenburg, Nova Scotia.

all 350 buildings in the district right down to the doorknobs. Of those 350 structures, 8 date from the eighteenth century, 50 from between 1800 and 1850, and a further 200 from 1860 to 1900, and all are made of wood, a remarkable celebration of urban heritage.

The town also adopted UNESCO's World Heritage Community Strategy by creating the Lunenburg World Heritage Community Foundation and Corporation in order to promote economic development, education, tourism, and heritage. Municipal and provincial grants and rebates followed to encourage private owners to adapt and preserve the heritage components of their respective properties.

The Heritage District encompasses the original grid layout and includes such structures as the 1770 courthouse (now the Anglican parish hall), the ancient churches, the old shipyard district, and the many vernacular-style wooden houses. In fact, as of 2008 more than sixty individual structures have been designated as heritage properties.

While Old Town Lunenburg still permits vehicles on its streets, it is ideal for walking. In fact, walking tours are available as guided tours or you can guide yourself with a brochure from the tourism centre, which is situated in a replica of the original blockhouse located beside Parade Square near the east end of town.

Along Bluenose Lane lies the town's maritime heritage. These include the inshore fishermen's wharf, the Fisheries Museum of the Atlantic, the *Bluenose* wharf, and the Fishermen's Memorial. This touching monument consists of granite columns dedicated to the 600 men lost on 150 ships. Its columns form a stylized compass rose. The most wrenching note on the memorial describes the 150 lives lost during a series of rare August gales in 1926 and 1927.

Farther along lies the Smith and Rhuland Shipyard, which launched the original *Bluenose*. Zwicker and Company dates back two hundred years and was the main shipper during the days of the salt cod, and the rum, sugar, and molasses trade with the West Indies. This working waterfront also includes Ocean Gear Company, which still makes rakes for the scallop draggers, next to which is Atlantic Electronics and Lunenburg Fish Company.

Walter's Blacksmith, established in 1893, is now the Ironworks Distillery, and the Dory Shop, which has been building dories for over a century and still builds custom wooden boats, encourages visitors to try their hand at building a dory of their own.

One block inland is Montague Street, along which are the many historic commercial buildings, most built of wood and brightly painted in colourful hues of orange, green, blue, and yellow.

Along the back streets, the visitor will encounter the many heritage houses, often displaying the iconic "Lunenburg bump" (essentially a second-storey bay window that extends over the porch). Several of these homes date back to the early 1800s.

Besides the churches, one of the most dramatic structures is the Lunenburg Academy, built in 1892 and Nova Scotia's last surviving academy.

Accommodation is available in many heritage inns, including the Rum Runners Inn, Smugglers Cove Inn, the Lunenburg Inn and Spa on Montague, and the grand Boscawen Inn situated on Lincoln Avenue on a hilltop overlooking the town.

Even outside the heritage zone, the town offers up more of its wonderful heritage. Dufferin Street, which leads west from the Old Town, displays a row of historic houses in a variety of vernacular styles.

Forgotten amid the town's overwhelming maritime legacy is the Lunenburg railway station, which now houses the Halifax and Southwestern Railway Museum. From the station, where the rails have long been lifted, the Bay to Bay Rail Trail leads around the peninsula to its north shore and to the Dynamite Rail Trail, which runs from Halifax to Yarmouth.

Lunenburg lies about a hundred kilometres west of Halifax just off Highway 103.

ST. ANDREWS BY-THE-SEA

Aside from the UNESCO sites, Canada can claim a number of historic townscapes. Situated in southern New Brunswick, on the shores of Passamaquoddy Bay, the historic town of St. Andrews by-the-Sea is a near twin to Lunenburg. Like Lunenburg, it occupies an eighteenth-century grid pattern town plan in the British colonial style. And, like Lunenburg, its early economy depended on shipping salted cod to the West Indies and lumber to England.

As the nineteenth century progressed, St. Andrews faded, its population shrinking to half its peak at the beginning of the century. Then, in the 1880s, the railways arrived, bringing in wealthy Americans from across the nearby border. Here, to escape the grime of their own cities, they built fine summer homes or booked into the grand resorts. After the CPR built its branch line from Macadam, New Brunswick, in 1889, the railway added the elegant chateau-style hotel the Algonquin Resort.

The town's economic stagnation proved a blessing in disguise, for it meant that its earliest and most historic stores and homes were not replaced by more modern styles.

In 1998 the Historic Sites and Monuments Board of Canada designated the entire town as a National Historic Site. *USA Today* has described St. Andrews as the "best destination in Canada," and in 2016 the Canadian Institute of Planners awarded the town its "Great Street" designation for Water Street's architectural heritage and preservation.

That street, which lines the shore, offers a variety of wooden shops and restaurants, while the residential streets boast nineteenth- and even eighteenth-century architectural styles.

Although trains no longer run, the Algonquin Resort, now much restored and rebuilt following a fire, still offers those luxury rooms as it has for more than a century. Today it is managed by Newcastle Hotels and Resorts.

William Cornelius Van Horne, the president of the CPR, was so taken by the town that he built his own summer estate on an island just offshore. Here, on the two-hundred-hectare Ministers Island, Van Horne built Covenhoven, a fifty-room cottage with eleven bathrooms and seventeen bedrooms (clearly, not all were en suite). His residence boasted running water, and nearby a massive turreted barn housed thoroughbred horses and Dutch Belted cattle. Accessible from the shore at low tide, the summer home was designed by Van Horne's key railway architect, Edward Maxwell, whose own "cottage" stands on the shore opposite the island. Tours of the property are offered during the summer months or upon appointment.

Many of Canada's towns and villages have, despite the unfortunate intrusion of megamalls and condos, managed to retain their heritage landscapes, even though in some cases they may have dwindled to ghost towns.

Often compared to Old Quebec, Kingston is called Ontario's City of Stone. As with towns along the Rideau Canal, many of its early buildings were built by the Scottish stonemasons who drudged on the canal. Kingston sits atop limestone deposits, which made that a logical building material. Many of that city's downtown shops and key structures, including the domed city hall, have inspired the label City of Stone. Sadly, however, Kingston's city council has a long history of disregarding this heritage in favour of the development industry, which continues to dangle the revenue of large-scale condo developments before their eyes.

Perth, on the other hand, has promoted its stone heritage with walking tours of Main Street and residential areas where some structures date to the early nineteenth century. Little wonder it has earned the title "Ontario's prettiest town." Situated on the Tay Canal, a branch of the Rideau Canal, it also benefited from the skills of the Scottish stonemasons.

The title of Ontario's "most historic town" has been awarded to Cobalt. Located in northeastern Ontario, it boomed from 1903 to 1930 as a silver boom town with dozens of silver mines, some right in the centre of town. Thanks to its rapid population decline from twenty thousand to one thousand, and despite a series of devastating fires, the town has retained many early boom-town buildings. New highways have passed the town by, bringing the urban sprawl and the unsightliness of the big-box world to nearby New Liskeard.

In northern Quebec, near Lac-Saint-Jean, the one-time mill town of Val-Jalbert is now a ghost town and is promoted as such. Created in 1901 at the foot of Ouiatchouan Falls for a pulp mill founded by Damase Jalbert, it closed in 1927. Its seventy buildings remained undisturbed in the remote woods, popular with photographers, until 1960 when the province of Quebec established a ghost town park to preserve the wooden structures, some repurposed for accommodation but most retained in a state of "suspended decay." It has been called "Canada's best-preserved ghost town."

Far to the north of Montreal, in the Abitibi region, the remarkable little community of Bourlamaque, while not a ghost town, is Canada's largest all-log community. Built in 1934 to house the workforce at the Lamaque gold mine at Val d'Or, the sixty-four log homes remain in their original condition and are now a provincial heritage district.

Vilna, Alberta, northeast of Edmonton, began in 1919 as a typical railway town, its grid street pattern stretching back from the tracks of the new Canadian National Railway. Along its main street were the usual array of stores and businesses, with their boom-town

The gold miners' community of Bourlamaque near Val d'Or in northern Quebec is North America's largest community constructed entirely of logs.

facades, including the popular pool hall along with the bank, hardware store, hotel, butcher shop, and post office. In 1999 Vilna received designation under Alberta's Main Street program to preserve its collection of main street buildings. Most sport the boom-town storefronts typical of early prairie railway towns. Few other prairie railway towns have been fortunate to retain an intact street such as that in Vilna. The 1921 combined pool hall and barber shop, both under the same roof, has been listed in the Canadian Registry of Historic Places.

TWENTY

FORTRESS OF LOUISBOURG: NORTH AMERICA'S LARGEST HISTORIC RE-CREATION

THE FORTRESS

The first look the visitor has of this massive reconstruction is one of awe. Here, on a barren point of land jutting into the windy Atlantic Ocean, sit massive stone walls that surround an entire eighteenth-century fortified French town. Except that the buildings here were built after 1961. A UNESCO World Heritage Site, Fortress of Louisbourg is North America's largest historic reconstruction project.

To be clear, a fortress is not the same thing as a fort. While the latter is a fortified military compound, a fortress is an entire fortified town.

For much of the eighteenth century, France and Great Britain waged war over their North American possessions. One of the many peace treaties that occasionally interrupted the fighting was the Treaty of Utrecht, signed in 1713. This one forced France to give up much of its North American maritime territory, keeping Île Royale (today's Cape Breton Island) and Île Saint-Jean (today's Prince Edward Island). To help defend their remaining territory, the French government undertook to construct a fortified town on the northeastern point of Cape Breton Island, where they could both protect vital

shipping lanes and establish a seat of government.

Construction began in 1719, and twenty years later the population stood at over two thousand, two-thirds of whom were civilians. The town included hotels, taverns, industries, and private homes, as well as a massive stone barracks and governor's house. Taking four years to construct, the four kilometres of walls measured ten metres high and twelve metres thick, and just to be safe, they added a moat. In its time, it was North America's largest fortified town. So much did it cost that King Louis XIV, after whom it was named, claimed that he had expected to be able to see it from France.

The ice-free harbour became a key port of call for merchant and naval ships as well as fishers, and it was vital in the cross-Atlantic and West Indies trading routes. In fact, it became the third-busiest port in North America.

However, the two warring nations were not quite finished fighting. The engineers who planned and built the fortress overlooked one thing. While the harbour side was well fortified, the land side was not. In 1744 war again erupted, and Britain captured the great fortress, occupying it for four years. That ended in 1748 when the Treaty of Aix-la-Chapelle returned the fortress to the French. As usual, the peace did not last, and in 1756 the two were at it again. When the British laid siege to Louisbourg in 1758, they captured the town once more. Then, after deporting Louisbourg's entire population back to France, the British demolished everything. Five years later, the Treaty of Paris ended France's presence in North America (with the exception of the tiny islands of Saint-Pierre and Miquelon off the coast of Newfoundland, which are still French territories).

For more than 150 years, the extensive field of ruins lay overgrown and open to the Atlantic winds. In 1928 the government of Canada declared the ruins a National Historic Site. Then, three decades later, to help bring tourism to a struggling Cape Breton, the government began what would become the largest historic reconstruction in North America and one of the largest in the world. The restoration would cost twenty-five million dollars and take six years to complete, while at the same time uncovering five and a half million artifacts.

Today's visitors will walk across a drawbridge and through the decorative Dauphin Gate to enter the walled town and walk back in time. Here, the road leads along the waterfront, passing guardhouses and an eighteenth-century-style latrine.

Not only is the town itself authentically re-created but so, too, are the many shops and homes. The bakery, modelled after the 1732 bakery, turns out genuine bread products. At the main corner, in the Hôtel de la Marine, liquid refreshments generally consisted of French wine and brandies, as rum and beer were rare commodities. The hotel today offers up soups and bread as well as eighteenth-century French food but may only provide a spoon for a utensil since early patrons would carry their own knives.

Opposite the hotel guarding the wharf is the elaborate Frédéric Gate. Beside the hotel sits a rum shop and rope-making business. A walk up the main street leads past more residences and ends at the King's Bastion, the massive military compound that housed the governor's offices and residence, the barracks for the officers and troops of the military, and a row of cannons.

Activities within the grounds are authentically re-created as well. "Soldiers" march in authentic uniforms, "citizens" wear period clothing, cannons in the fort blast away at regular intervals, while an unfortunate "prisoner" may be seen languishing in the stockade. Visitors are also invited to relive the lifestyle of the eighteenth century, employing early farming techniques and learning to fire a musket or even a cannon. Rum tasting offers adults a taste of the past, and the adventurous may camp overnight under the stunning star-filled skies.

Incredibly, the extensive re-creation takes in only one-quarter of the original fortress. Beyond the standing structures, paths lead through the massive field of foundations and ruins, many of which have plaques to indicate their original use.

Today the entire site remains remote and windswept. While a paved road leads from the current tourist town of Louisbourg itself, the fortress, with its desolate location and realistic re-creations, presents as genuine a visit to the past as one will find in North America.

Cape Breton's Fortress of Louisbourg, a massive Parks Canada re-creation of an eighteenth-century French fortress, is a World Heritage Site and one of Cape Breton's main tourist destinations.

THE FORTS

Forts that have been restored or replicated are found in most provinces, the greatest concentration being in eastern Canada, where many early wars were fought. The star-shaped Halifax Citadel dates from 1856. The fourth such structure on the high hill, it was designated a National Historic Site in 1935. For many years it remained a crumbling ruin, inviting threats of demolition from the Halifax business community anxious to accommodate more parking (a sad but familiar story). Finally, the city began to recognize its value as a tourist attraction and opened it for tours in 1956.

The reconstruction of the massive Citadel of Quebec began in 1820 and was completed in 1831. The star-shaped ramparts enclose North America's largest British fortress, including an earlier French military structure from 1693, and it remains home to the Royal Twenty-Second Regiment of the Canadian Armed Forces. It became a National Historic Site in 1980 and forms part of the UNESCO World Heritage Site of Quebec City.

In Kingston, Old Fort Henry, built in 1831–37 in part to defend the southern entrance to the Rideau Canal and the British naval dockyards nearby, is Canada's largest fortification outside of Quebec City. After 1891 it no longer saw military service and fell into ruin.

Restoration began in 1936, and two years later the fort was opened as a tourist attraction. The fort served as a prisoner-of-war camp during both world wars, after which the tourists began to return. Today it is one of the city's longest-running tourist attractions with its military drills and summer orchestra performances. Along with a string of round forts called Martello towers, it is part of the UNESCO Rideau Canal and Kingston Fortifications World Heritage Site.

Meanwhile, in Toronto, Fort York contains Canada's largest collection of original War of 1812 military buildings, having replaced an earlier fort near the same site. Now set back from the lake due to several landfill operations, it survived a determined bid to relocate it for the building of the Gardiner Expressway.

Perhaps the one fort that is unlike any other in North America is Prince of Wales Fort in Churchill, Manitoba. That is partially because, due to its remoteness, it is nearly inaccessible. When the Hudson's Bay Company began expanding across northern Canada in the 1670s, an area called Rupert's Land, they needed a sturdy fort to defend the mouth of the Churchill River on Hudson Bay, a strategic location in the fur trade, against possible French attack.

Construction began in the 1730s and took nearly forty years to complete. The short duration of the construction season and the need to hunt and gather endless supplies of wood meant that speedy progress was impossible. The fort bore the usual military star shape, with outer walls 6.5 metres high and 15 metres thick. But it lacked the manpower for its forty-two

Troops of the Fort York Guard on parade at Old Fort York, Ontario. A fort was established at this site in 1793 to help protect Upper Canada from American invasion. The original fort was destroyed in 1813 during the War of 1812; the present fort was built soon afterward.

cannons. In 1782 the French attacked and handily captured the fort, destroying many of the buildings.

It remained in ruins even in 1920, when the National Historic Sites and Monuments Board of Canada (in those days obsessed with all things military) declared it a National Historic Site. In the 1930s, with the completion of the railway to Churchill, the government began much-needed repairs. Now partially back to its original form, it attracts curious visitors from around the globe who otherwise come to the remote port of Churchill to gaze on its population of polar bears.

Canada's early military legacy can be found in many other smaller fortifications across the country, many of which are replications, but none can match the Fortress of Louisbourg.

TWENTY-ONE

HO! FOR THE KLONDIKE

THE GOLDEN STAMPEDE

What is it about the allure of gold that drives men (and some women) to do almost anything to find the motherlode? Ever since early humans learned how to form metals into decorative shapes, gold has been the most eagerly sought. It drove the Spanish in their futile quest to seek out a legendary city of gold they called Eldorado; it also led them to destroy the ancient Aztec and Incan empires in the 1520s and 1530s.

In Canada, the earliest metal to be mined and exploited was copper. It was a soft metal and relatively easy to extract and shape. Indigenous Peoples found it in quantity along the north shore of Lake Huron and the south shore of Lake Superior and used it for trading. Gold, however, was much harder to extract and was usually found only in the form of dust in riverbeds, nuggets, or veins in hard rock. But it had the greatest allure.

Egyptian kings and queens formed stunning sceptres, maces, jewellery, and even burial masks from the precious metal.

It was one of the many valuables that drove European traders and explorers to seek the all-important shortcut to Asia. When they were blocked by the North American continent, they decided to plunder the riches of Central and South America.

Gold seekers would do nearly anything to find it, enduring remarkable hardships and even tempting death to seek it out.

In North America, Europeans launched gold rushes in places as unlikely as Georgia, while similarly in Canada, the earliest gold rush in Ontario took place a short distance north of Lake Ontario. Here, the discovery of a golden nugget in 1866 lured prospectors to found a boom town they called Eldorado. When the deposits proved too small, too difficult to extract, or even nonexistent, the town became a ghost town. And for the most part, it still is.

As the American frontier moved inexorably westward, prospectors discovered gold in California, and the rush of 1849 was on. Then, as the deposits became exhausted, the gold seekers turned their attention to wherever the cry of "gold" was heard, leaving boom towns to die. One of the best examples is the preserved ghost town of Bodie in California, now a state park.

North of the border, in British Columbia, gold was discovered in 1858 along the turbulent Fraser River, and the "forty-niners" streamed northward, giving rise to boom towns like Yale and Lillooet. They then moved north into the Cariboo country, giving rise to the historic ghost town of Barkerville, preserved as a historic park.

Gold had long been suspected to exist in the Yukon. Until 1878 the local Indigenous inhabitants kept prospectors at bay. In that year prospector George Holt found gold, and within two years two hundred eager gold seekers converged on the scene from as far away as Circle City, Alaska.

Still, it wasn't until 1885 that gold was found in any quantity, at Forty Mile on the Yukon River.

For the most part, however, the motherlode remained elusive — that is, until 1896 when a prospector named Robert Henderson shared news of a discovery, as was the tradition among prospectors, with an old forty-niner named George Carmack. Henderson, though, refused to have anything to do with Carmack's First Nations partners, Skookum Jim and Tagish Charlie.

The trio then decided to follow Henderson's lead, and they found in the nearby bed of Rabbit Creek sizeable nuggets, enough to send them scurrying in to Forty Mile to stake their claim. Because of Henderson's slighting of his Indigenous partners, Carmack ignored the standard protocol of sharing the news with him.

Hearing news of the discovery, local prospectors descended on Rabbit Creek, quickly renaming it Eldorado Creek, and had soon staked all the best claims.

Having loaded their sacks with their golden bounty, they chomped at the bit to return home to show it off, but that would mean waiting until the shipping season opened the following spring.

On July 4, 1897, at San Francisco, thousands of curious onlookers, hearing of the gold strike, crowded the steamer dock as the SS *Excelsior* manoeuvred into position. On board, the grizzled (and likely unwashed) miners hauled off the boat gold that was worth one to two million dollars, or seventy million dollars in 2018, as gold was valued at twenty dollars an ounce in 1896. On July 14, the SS *Portland* arrived at Seattle carrying another million dollars in gold, worth thirty-five million dollars in 2018.

With the continent in an economic depression, the mad scramble began. Throngs invaded the outfitter stores to get stoves, coats, boots, picks, and backpacks, and, along with hundreds of horses and mules, they crammed on board any vessel that remained afloat.

By late summer and early fall, nearly a hundred thousand anxious gold seekers from all corners of the continent, and even from overseas, were on their way to the Klondike. Many carried outlandish luggage like chairs, tables, wardrobes, and even a grand piano, all on their way to reap the gold that lined the streets of Forty Mile, which would soon be renamed Dawson City.

Or so they thought.

Still, it was the beginning of one of the largest gold stampedes the world has ever witnessed. And its ghosts linger to this day.

The stampede began with unbridled enthusiasm. After weeks of suffering seasickness on cramped, lurching vessels, the stampeders' first shock came

Parks Canada and the U.S. National Parks Service have jointly reopened the challenging Chilkoot Trail, which once led prospectors to the legendary Klondike goldfields. Most turned back before getting there. Trail-side shelters today make the journey somewhat less arduous.

when the boats grounded themselves on the vast and muddy tidal flats that extended out from the ramshackle Alaskan boom towns of Dyea and Skagway. The latter marked the start of the White Pass Trail, the former that of the shorter Chilkoot Trail, both of which led to the goldfields.

The next shock came in discovering that Skagway was literally a den of thieves led by a notorious con artist named "Soapy" Smith, who pocketed millions of dollars by fleecing gullible Klondikers with a range of nefarious illegal schemes. He would be shot dead a year later.

After experiencing the initial trauma of what lay before them, most climbed back on board the frail steamers and returned home. Of the hundred thousand who started out, fewer than half forged on.

Both trails held daunting perils. The White Pass Trail from Skagway seemed to be the gentler route, a misconception that would prove fatally deceptive. The line of horses moved achingly slowly, if at all. Pack animals by the hundreds died along its narrow, steep, and boulder-strewn trail, some of exhaustion, others from munching on poisonous plants, until the route became known as the Dead Horse Trail. None of the wretched animals made it to the summit.

While the Chilkoot Trail from Dyea was steeper and more perilous, a greater percentage of trekkers surmounted that summit than did those who made it over the lower White Pass.

And what a summit it was. For there before them stood a forty-five-degree wall of rock and snow, and they had to get their tonne of supplies over it or the Mounties stationed at the border post at the summit would turn them back. Most had to make forty trips up the snowy slope.

But that wasn't the end of it. Beyond the pass, although the trail mercifully levelled to the shores of Bennett Lake, there lay another eight hundred kilometres to the goldfields. Here, on the shores of the lake, the gold seekers had to endure the brutal winter as each group had to make their own boat to cross the lake and navigate the churning Yukon River.

After each obstacle the group got ever smaller, and only ten thousand managed to complete the entire journey. At this point they were greeted with their final shock: the reality that the golden riverbeds had all been staked.

So great was the demand for products and accommodation that many turned their time to opening hotels and shops. A few worked for miners on their existing claims. Dance halls like that run by the legendary Diamond Tooth Gertie became icons of the area. Other women decided to sell their personal services to lonely miners in exchange for their gold. Ironically, it was a trade that the Mounties tolerated even though Sunday work was forbidden. Firearms were prohibited. Unlike the raucous American mining towns, Dawson witnessed not a single murder.

Of the famous gold discoverers, Tagish Charlie died broke and an alcoholic, Skookum Jim headed off in search of more golden riches and was never heard from again, and George Carmack invested in real estate in Vancouver and died a wealthy man in 1922.

Another entrepreneur, who also had an interest in real estate, was the German-born Friedrich Trump. Lured to the Klondike by way of New York, he arrived at Bennett Lake, where, according to Gwenda Blair, author of *The Trumps: Three Generations That Built an Empire*, he opened his New Arctic Restaurant. Here, he offered the Klondikers horse meat, oysters, and caribou as well as (allegedly) flesh of a different kind — that of his ladies. With the end of the boom times in Bennett Lake, and with the opening of the White Pass and Yukon Railway to Whitehorse, he relocated to the new town of Whitehorse and opened a similar enterprise there. Facing a police crackdown on such establishments, he fled back to Germany, where he was deported as a draft dodger and returned to New York.

There, in that booming city, with his ill-gotten gains from the Klondike, he launched a real estate empire that his grandson would ultimately inherit … that heir being one Donald Trump.

Despite the disappointments in Dawson, gold fever refused to abate, and by 1900 a new frenzy lured prospectors to Nome, Alaska. Notwithstanding the drastic decline in Dawson's population and the loss of many buildings to fire, the golden age was not quite over. Larger industrial gold extraction moved in with monster dredgers, scooping the riverbeds and washing away the gravel.

Despite the dredges, by the 1950s Dawson City's population had plummeted to only a few hundred. The city had become a ghost town.

Then, in 1959, thanks in part to a National Film Board documentary called *City of Gold*, narrated by Dawson-born Pierre Berton, the government of Canada created a National Historic complex within Dawson and declared the town a National Historic Site.

The gold rush was said to be the most photographed event in North America, and more than two hundred photos appear in Berton's book *The Klondike Quest*. However, it was Berton's mother, Laura, who provided an intimate look into life in the gold town as a twenty-five-year-old schoolteacher with her own memoir, *I Married the Klondike*. Berton's Dawson house is now known as the Writers' Block, a retreat for working writers.

Parks Canada then began to restore some of Dawson City's more important buildings and today administers twenty-five such properties, including the former paddlewheeler the SS *Keno*, the Palace Grand Theatre, Madame Tremblay's store, the post office, and the former Territorial Administration Building, which now houses the Dawson City Museum. This facility offers stories of the golden age, costumes, and a shelter housing the steam locomotives that shuttled between the goldfields and the steamer dock.

Many others, such as the former gambling and dance hall owned by Diamond Tooth Gertie, are preserved privately. Today, complete with cancan dancers, it claims the title as Canada's oldest gambling hall.

Dawson City is a ghost town no longer. Its population has rebounded from fewer than 700 in 1981, tripling to more than 2,100 in 2016. Boarded up and collapsing buildings no longer line its streets, although a few of those yet linger. Now more than fifty businesses and accommodations provide the economic base for the town, many of them built in the traditional boom town–style.

While most of the original boom-town buildings are now gone, enough of the town's golden heritage remains to attract thousands of tourists each summer. Some will visit the Discovery Site on Bonanza Creek and tour the massive remains of Dredge Number 4. They may seek out their own gold in the many gift shops or by panning the creeks for the priceless gold dust. Some might even find some.

An important stop is the Dänojà Zho Cultural Centre, which tells the story of the region's earliest inhabitants, the Tr'ondëk Hwëch'in Peoples, whose lands and resources became the victims of gold fever.

Accommodation and guided tours are plentiful. While many of the back streets now boast more modern homes and structures, there remain enough boom town–style buildings to evoke those heady days of the great Klondike gold rush. A few, however, remain derelict, with the town council seriously pondering their fate. Despite the unique value of these aging structures, the town may place the costs of saving them against the benefits of tearing them down to make way for more building lots and thus more municipal revenues. Sadly, it is a fate that threatens much of Canada's underappreciated built heritage.

Commercial gold production itself has not disappeared entirely either. While it no longer achieves the level of more than one million ounces a year as it did in 1900, production over the last forty years has ranged between fifty thousand and a hundred thousand ounces a year.

The Road to Riches Today

Those not content to merely visit this legendary city of gold can follow in the historic footsteps of the Klondikers. Literally. Now maintained jointly by Parks Canada and the U.S. National Parks Service, the legendary Chilkoot Trail still leads from the site of the muddy Dyea, over the Golden Staircase of the summit, and to the shores of Bennett Lake.

For safety reasons, the authorities will allow only fifty hikers a day to embark on the fifty-three-kilometre trek. Travelling in groups of four, they must register in Skagway before setting out.

From Skagway, with its historic main street still lined with boom-town structures, a dirt road winds its way to the ghost town of Dyea, although no buildings still stand. Many of the same hardships that faced the Klondikers still face today's travellers: steep slopes, muddy creeks, vertigo, and boulder-strewn paths. The path is marked but not maintained. The only amenity consists of shelters with cookstoves strategically located at the end of each day's hike.

Still, the Golden Staircase remains the most daunting obstacle on the route, but once across it is a relatively level path to the once-bustling tent city of Bennett on the shores of Bennett Lake.

Today that once-booming place is a ghost town as well, with only a few artifacts strewn about (which cannot be tampered with), the iconic wooden Saint Andrews Presbyterian Church being the sole surviving gold rush structure.

Another welcoming sight in Bennett is the immaculately maintained White Pass and Yukon Railway station. This two-storey red wooden station offers shelter for hikers and some refreshment as well, for from here the only way back out is by train. The trip may take the hiker back to Skagway or farther along to an identical railway station at Carcross, which is road accessible. A bus operates from there into Whitehorse.

In 1899 the White Pass and Yukon Railway opened from Skagway to Whitehorse, replacing the White Pass Trail. From Whitehorse, steamers would carry the passengers downriver to Dawson. While today's excursion trains no longer travel to Whitehorse, the large log station in that city has now been put to other uses. Close by lies the SS *Kaslo* paddlewheeler, which once took passengers from the station there to Dawson.

Using historic railway equipment, day-long train excursions operate from Skagway. After rising a thousand metres in just thirty kilometres, the tracks lead to the identical two-storey stations at Bennett and Carcross. Running daily from May 2 to September 28, the three-and-a-half-hour round trip operates two or three times a day and may include steam engine trips for a shorter distance to the Fraser station.

Finally, for those "Cheechakoes" (the Klondike term for outsiders) who prefer the luxury of the car, the modern Klondike Highway leads from Skagway for 715 kilometres to Dawson.

This route leaves the historic main street of Skagway, which has retained or replicated its boom town–style structures, including the attractive wooden WP&Y railway station with its high-ceilinged waiting room.

Completed in 1978, the highway, numbered Highway 98 in Alaska and Highway 2 after it enters Canada, passes Skagway's Gold Rush Cemetery, which contains the grave marker for one J.R. "Soapy" Smith. For 22.5 kilometres, the highway rises more than a thousand metres before reaching the Canadian border. At Carcross, the road passes along the small main street where the WP&Y station stands across from the historic Matthew Watson General Store and one-time hotel. Here, too, lies the world's smallest "desert," a sandy former glacial lake bottom of only 260 hectares.

Seventy-four kilometres from Carcross, the road reaches Whitehorse, and from here Highway 2 roughly parallels the Yukon River for 533 kilometres to the Klondike. Services along it are spaced far apart.

On this portion of the route, it passes the famous Five Finger Rapids that plagued the early gold seekers in their makeshift vessels. Eventually, the road reaches the Bonanza Creek Discovery Claim historic site, the place where it all began. Here, too, is Dredge Number 4, one of the world's largest gold dredges and itself a National Historic Site. A few kilometres later, the highway enters the boom-town streets of Dawson City, once one of the largest cities west of Chicago.

While the region today enjoys air service and paved highways, it is still not easy to get to. The highways are long and often lacking in services, and air travel remains pricey. Winter temperatures can plunge to as low as minus fifty degrees Celsius, and extended periods of daily darkness mean that the area, for most southerners, remains pretty much a seasonal destination, which also shows how challenging the Klondike quest must surely have been for the gold-seeking thousands of more than a century ago.

The Klondike was not Canada's first golden stampede. Not too surprisingly, British Columbia's best-preserved ghost town stems from the Cariboo gold rush of the 1850s. Owned by the province and managed as a heritage property and park, Barkerville contains 107 preserved heritage buildings, including much of the original Chinatown, and 65 replica structures. It was founded in 1862 following the discovery of gold by Billy Barker on Keithley Creek. By the 1880s its population had boomed to five thousand, half of whom were Chinese. With others streaming in from Australia, Europe, and Mexico, including black Americans and local First Nations

The Cariboo gold rush town of Barkerville in British Columbia's interior has been preserved as a ghost town park, North America's most extensive.

Peoples, Barkerville had become one of the largest cities in western Canada and one of its most diverse.

Even after the federal government declared the site a National Historic Site in 1923, it continued to produce gold, with its last permanent resident dying in 1979. It became a provincial heritage site in 1958. Today it is claimed to be the largest heritage site in western North America.

TWENTY-TWO

CANADA'S ELUSIVE NORTHWEST PASSAGE

The world's most elusive passageway, which for centuries eluded navigators searching for that vital route to the riches of China, lurked around the north end of Canada: the fabled and fatal Northwest Passage.

When Marco Polo had returned from his twenty-year stay in China in 1299, with his stories of fabulous spices and satins, the merchants and monarchs of Europe decided to find a way to the east. Sea routes around the tips of Africa and South America proved dangerous and deadly. There had to be a better way.

Christopher Columbus tried it in 1492 but found himself in the maze of islands that he mistakenly called the West "Indies," believing at first that he had reached that eastern land. Balboa tried it, too, but found the Isthmus of Panama in the way, which he crossed only to find that another ocean, the Pacific, lay before him. This led many Europeans to believe that North America was only a narrow impediment, and so they decided to try the northern route.

While the Vikings had settled briefly in northern Newfoundland, they were seeking Vineland, not China. North of that lay the Arctic Archipelago, a maze of islands, channels, and dead ends, a labyrinth of barren rocks and ice-clogged waterways. Here,

surely, lay the Northwest Passage and the route to the riches of the East.

Among the first to try was Martin Frobisher in 1576, but he couldn't penetrate beyond Baffin Island. In 1578 he was sent off again, this time with fifteen ships and the intention to establish a mining colony in the Arctic. After losing many of his ships, he returned to England carrying nothing but a pile of worthless black rocks that he had thought may contain gold.

He was followed by John Davis in 1585, 1586, and 1587, but he sailed south into the dead end of Hudson Bay. Although convinced that the "passage" lay north of Baffin Island, he, too, sailed back to England.

Next up was Henry Hudson. After vainly seeking a route to the east by travelling north of Russia, and one south from Newfoundland, he, too, decided to give Hudson Bay a try. In July 1610 he set sail with the *Discovery*.

In September 1611 the *Discovery* returned to England but with no Hudson on board. He, too, had entered the bay that now carries his name, but his crew, tired of his imperious ways, set him and his son and a few loyal crew members adrift in a small boat, never to be seen again.

The few mutineers who survived the ordeal escaped the noose when the ship's navigator, Robert Bylot, claimed that they had, in fact, discovered the passage. In 1616 Bylot was given the chance to prove it and set off with William Baffin. Although he failed to locate the passage, he at least realized that the route lay north of Baffin Island through Lancaster Sound and not through Hudson Bay.

Then, in 1619, Danish Norwegian Jens Munk set off with two ships and sixty-four men. Two years later he sailed back with only a single vessel and four starving crew. The rest had died from eating undercooked polar bear meat, a fate that was later thought to have decimated most of the crew who accompanied John Franklin on his ill-fated effort to locate the passage.

Discouraged by the repeated failures, commercial interests then shifted to the fine furs that Canada's North produced, and in 1670 King Charles II granted a charter to the Hudson's Bay Company. The newly formed company set up base in the large bay named after Captain Henry Hudson, where they created a string of trading posts. Their monopoly extended to the entire Hudson Bay watershed, including all the rivers that drained into it.

Interest in the Northwest Passage soon resurfaced when James Knight, a Hudson's Bay factor, heard of a passage through the Arctic where lay stories of gold. After Knight set sail from England on an expedition in 1719, he disappeared from the record. In 1819 William Perry gave it a shot, followed by John Franklin, who hoped to find a west-to-east route in 1819–22 and again in 1825–27. But the surging mountains of ice thwarted all efforts.

By 1845 John Franklin had become a well-respected Arctic explorer and navigator, and in that year the British colonial office outfitted him for a major search for the elusive waterway. With two ships, the *Terror* and the *Erebus*, and a crew of 129, loaded with provisions for a three-year expedition, including two thousand books, several thousand litres of liquor, and a piano, Franklin set sail.

And was never heard from again.

By 1848 his expedition was presumed lost, and the admiralty, urged on by Franklin's determined wife, Jane, launched thirty search expeditions over an eleven-year period.

While some evidence was recovered in that time, including buttons and other small artifacts, it was James Penny's discovery of three graves, dated 1846, on Beechey Island in 1850, and then in 1859, Francis McClure's discovery of a cairn on King William Island, that further confirmed the fate of the voyage. In that cairn was a logbook that described the death of Franklin on June 11, 1847, and the decision to abandon ship the following year. The ships had been stuck fast in ice for three years. Eventually, the pressure of the ice buckled the hulls, and the vessels sank into a then unknown grave.

Oral history of local Inuit describes emaciated crew members hauling their lifeboats across the frozen wasteland.

However, the expeditions were all looking in the wrong place. Their main focus had been to travel across the north of Baffin Island and then straight west through the Lancaster Sound and Viscount Melville Channel. On the maps, it appeared to offer a wide lane straight to the Beaufort Sea, the western end of the passage. However, that passage was constantly blocked with ice migrating south from the polar ice cap, forcing ships to steer south down the west side of Somerset Island and the Boothia Peninsula.

They would then make their way down the west side of King William Island, which they had mistakenly believed to be a peninsula, and into the impenetrable path of the ice floes. It is here that Franklin's ships became permanently trapped.

Oddly, it was an overland exploration by a Hudson's Bay Company surgeon named Dr. John Rae in 1854 that first identified that the King William "peninsula" was, in fact, an island, and that another route, the relatively ice-free missing link, lay between it and the mainland.

Meanwhile, it had gradually dawned on Lady Franklin and the British Admiralty that Franklin and his crew were dead. In the following years, Lady Franklin refused to acknowledge that Rae was the legitimate discoverer of the Northwest Passage and instead lobbied the British government to erect a large statue claiming that her late husband, in fact, deserved the credit for that discovery, while Rae was largely vilified. Even today the British government refuses to acknowledge this injustice.

However, Rae's Scottish supporters have erected a statue in his honour in Stromness, his hometown. In modern times, 1999, Arctic expert Ken McGoogan along with Cameron Treleaven and Inuit historian Louie Kamookak erected a plaque honouring Rae on the Boothia Peninsula overlooking Rae Strait and

next to the remains of a cairn that Rae himself had built in 1854.

It was Rae's discovery that led a Danish explorer, Roald Amundsen, to try following the narrow channels closer to the mainland. After wintering in a harbour that he called Gjoa (pronounced "Joe" and named after his ship) Haven in 1903–05, on the southeast coast of King William Island, he set off through Rae's passage and hugged the coastline south of the large Victoria Island, which led him to his destination, the Beaufort Sea.

His voyages took him three years, but at last he had made it through the elusive passage, the first to ever do so. After completing his historic trip, he exonerated Rae, acknowledging that it was the Hudson's Bay Company doctor who should be credited with identifying the true route of the passage. The British, though, remained unimpressed.

It ultimately took a Canadian, Henry Larsen of the RCMP, to become the first to complete the voyage in a single year when in 1940 he sailed the *St. Roch* into the Beaufort Sea and then back again in 1942. Two years after that, with a heavier engine and ship, he managed to navigate a different route straight through Lancaster Sound and the Viscount Melville Channel farther north.

With the passage traversed, there remained one thing to do: find Franklin's ships. Inuit had always claimed that their oral tradition placed the doomed ships to the west of King William Island. In fact, even in recent times, some had observed what appeared to be a ship's mast still protruding above the waters.

Following that lead, and with painstaking underwater research by Parks Canada, the Arctic Research

Foundation, and the Royal Canadian Geographic Society, and equipped with technology provided by One Ocean Expeditions, the wreck of the *Erebus* was found in 2014, roughly where Inuit had described it to be a century and a half earlier.

Below the clear, chilly waters off King William Island, they saw the remarkably preserved vessel. Two years later near Terror Bay, the *Terror*, too, was located. Both may reveal many of the mysteries of their fates and those of the crew as well. Both locations are now National Historic Sites, and the seabeds around them have been declared off limits to the public to protect the sites from possible salvagers. To ensure no one interferes with these archaeological prizes, the government has engaged local Inuit to guard the sites, while a number of Canadian security

The Arctic community of Gjoa Haven began when Roald Amundsen sought shelter there on his way to the Northwest Passage.

agencies, including the RCMP and the Coast Guard, monitor the area.

Over the years, global warming has shrunk the ice pack to the point that, in 1969, a massive ice-breaking oil tanker, the SS *Manhattan*, was able to penetrate the route.

Today the Northwest Passage has become a popular cruise destination. While most cruise ships are small and do not follow in the exact footsteps of Amundsen or Larsen, they do visit many of the historic locations and take in the rugged, soaring coastlines that the earliest navigators would have experienced.

THE ROUTE TODAY

Aside from the itineraries of the cruise lines, a virtual tour of the Northwest Passage may be charted. It could well start at Cartwright, Newfoundland and Labrador, the only highway access to the east end of the passage, lying at the end of the Trans-Labrador Highway 516.

The sea route would then follow the Labrador coast, where islands with such names as Blowhard, Graveyard, Coffin, and Cutthroat suggest a challenging region to navigate. Tucked into the bays and inlets, several Inuit settlements offer sanctuary.

The route leads to the northern tip of Quebec, where the Torngat Mountains National Park shows off soaring, craggy coastal cliffs, some rising a kilometre above the grey seas and displaying rocks that are among the oldest on earth.

Just to the north of the Torngats lies one of the Arctic Archipelago's largest islands, Baffin Island, with the city of Iqaluit, the capital of the recently created separate territory of Nunavut. The first European to enter Baffin Bay was Martin Frobisher in 1576, thinking this to be the fabled passage to China. He was wrong not only on that count but also in thinking he had found gold, which proved to be only pyrite, also known as fool's gold.

Throughout the nineteenth century, the site hosted a whaling station, a Hudson's Bay Company post, and church missions. In the 1920s it became an RCMP outpost, and during the Second World War it was a U.S. air base. Later, during the Cold War, it formed part of the Distant Early Warning defence line or DEW line. It was known at the time as Frobisher Bay.

As the community continued to grow, it became an important federal government site, attracting increasing numbers of scattered Inuit populations. After the Americans pulled out, the community grew into an almost fully Inuit community and in 1999 became the capital of the new Nunavut territory, reclaiming its Inuktitut name of Iqaluit, meaning "place of fish."

Unlike in the days of the early explorers, Iqaluit today offers amenities such as accommodations, secondary and postsecondary schools, and a museum, and it has a surprisingly diverse population, boasting a Muslim mosque and restaurant, the Yummy Shawarma. It has more recently become a port of call for the cruise ships.

Cape Dorset, another popular port of call, is renowned for artwork and crafts of local Inuit. Settlement in this area dates back more than two thousand years to the Dorset peoples. Vikings are believed to have visited in 1000 CE. In 1913, the Hudson's Bay Company opened a busy post here, and the location began to attract more permanent residents. Thanks to early artists, Cape Dorset has grown into a noted producer of Inuit carvings and art.

Along the north coast of Baffin Island lie a string of communities and the spectacularly rugged Auyuittuq and Sirmilik National Parks. Mount Thor, officially called the Thor Peak, in Auyuittuq National Park, is the world's tallest purely vertical drop. From its granite peak, the drop measures 1,250 metres and angles inward at 105 degrees, making it more of an overhang.

It is to the west of here that the vestiges of failed expeditions lurk. On a windswept beach on Beechey Island lie the graves of three sailors from the Franklin expedition as well as that of a sailor from the 1850 McClure expedition, one of many sent to discover the fate of Franklin (whom many believed might still be alive even then).

Bronze plaques on the aging wooden grave markers list the dead as Chief Petty Officer John Torrington, age twenty, Royal Marine Private William Braine, age thirty-two, Able Seaman John Hartnell, age twenty-five, all from the Franklin ships, and Thomas Morgan, age thirty, from the McClure expedition.

Four lonely graves on remote Beechey Island in Canada's Arctic Archipelago remind visitors of the tragic fate of John Franklin's search for the Northwest Passage.

In 1981 a team of anthropologists from the University of Alberta exhumed the bodies and confirmed that starvation and lead poisoning were the causes of their deaths. (The source of the lead, however, was not the cans of meat that the crew took with them, as earlier scientists had believed, but rather toxins released in their bodies due to eating undercooked polar bear meat.) Cut marks on the bones also confirmed what Inuit had long claimed, and what the Franklin searchers failed to accept, that the corpses were also the victims of cannibalism.

In 1927 a pair of renowned artists from the Group of Seven artists' collective, Lawren Harris and A.Y. Jackson, toured the Northwest Passage and brought the Franklin legacy to their art. While Harris sketched the barren landscapes of Bylot Island, Jackson did manage to incorporate part of the Franklin legacy into his sketch of Beechey Island. Here, one of the Franklin searchers, Captain John Ross, had left on the shore of the island his small vessel, the *Mary*, loaded with a cache of supplies in the unlikely chance that Franklin might yet encounter it. In 1927 Jackson captured the remains of the *Mary* in his sketch *The* Mary *at the Foot of the Cliff, Beechey Island, 1927.*

Then, in 2012, Group of Seven researchers Jim and Sue Waddington noted in their book *In the Footsteps of the Group of Seven* that little remained of the vessel at the site, save a few nails and rotting lumber.

From Beechey Island, the Northwest Passage then turns south down the Franklin Strait, passing between Prince of Wales Island and Somerset Island.

On Somerset stands an abandoned Hudson's Bay Company trading post built in 1937 and closed a decade later. At the foot of the strait, on the ice-clogged west side of King William Island, lies the final resting place of Franklin's ships.

In 1903 Amundsen followed Rae's observations and took the channel to the east of King William Island, where he spent the first of his three winters readying his ship, the *Gjoa*, for his final push into the passage, founding the community of Gjoa Haven. By the time the Hudson's Bay Company opened a post in 1928, the community had a population of only 110. Today that population numbers nearly 1,500 (95 percent are Inuit).

To commemorate its Northwest Passage heritage, the community has created the Northwest Passage Territorial Trail, with heritage signs that recount the stories of the futile searches for the lost Franklin expedition as well as the days in 1903–05 when Roald Amundsen stayed there while preparing for the world's first traverse of the passage.

The trail also takes in the community's oldest structure, namely the original Hudson's Bay Company trading post, and then leads out of the hamlet to a cairn dedicated to Amundsen. Here, too, are the mounds and pits from the buildings that Amundsen erected before continuing on his voyage to the west.

Amundsen's route then passed south of King William Island, following Rae's channel, then south of Victoria Island and through the Dease Strait into the Amundsen Gulf on the Beaufort Sea. Here, today's community of Ulukhaktok (formerly Holman) is noted for its printmaking, carvings, traditional hats made of qiviut (muskox wool), and ulus, the half-round knives traditionally used in skinning animals.

Once into the Beaufort Sea, the last leg of the Northwest Passage, Herschel Island, which Franklin mapped coming from the west in the 1820s, contains the remains of a whaling station and evidence of the early Thule culture. It is also the only location where three types of bear are found together: black, grizzly, and polar. Here, too, global warming is eroding the shorelines at a more rapid rate than anywhere else on earth due to wave action from the now ice-free waters. Global warming, too, is reducing the ice cover across the Arctic to the point that the Northwest Passage will no longer be the obstacle that for centuries turned back every effort to unlock its mysteries and sealed the fate of many mariners. And that might not be a good thing.

In November 2017 a 138-kilometre-long all-season road was opened to link Inuvik to Tuktoyaktuk, meaning that now not only is the country finally linked by road from "sea to sea to sea" but also that both the east and west ends of the Northwest Passage are now accessible by road.

TWENTY-THREE

THE RIDEAU CANAL:
A WATERWAY FROM THE PAST

THE CANAL

There is little wonder why in 2007 UNESCO inscribed the Rideau Canal and Kingston Fortifications as a World Heritage Site. It is quite simply North America's oldest continuously operating canal, and its many features, both structural and military, reflect that distinctive heritage.

Its roots date to the War of 1812, during which time the British army in Canada along with Kanien'keha:ka allies and local militias fought to stave off numerous attacks from the expansion-minded Americans, and they succeeded in doing so. To avoid future threats to their military operations, the British decided to move their main water route from the vulnerable St. Lawrence River to a more secure location farther inland.

In 1826 the British sent Lieutenant Colonel John By of the Corps of Royal Engineers into a mosquito-infested wilderness between Lake Ontario and the Ottawa River to determine the best route. By concluded that rather than carve out a long trench through the wilderness, he would instead use the region's natural waterways, damming the many lakes and rivers and linking them with a series of locks.

Work began in 1827 with an original cost estimate of sixty-two thousand pounds. Over a period of five difficult years, six thousand labourers, predominantly Irish and French Canadian, along with local blacksmiths and Scottish stonemasons, toiled in swamps, with hundreds dying from malaria in that time. Their only equipment were horses and human muscle. Rocks were quarried from nearby sites and hauled by horse to the lock stations.

By the time By inaugurated the new canal by travelling from Kingston to Ottawa in 1832, his achievement was widely acclaimed as a true engineering marvel. Unfortunately, it was also wildly over budget, having ballooned to more than eight hundred thousand pounds. For that, By was put on trial in England, while his remarkable accomplishment was ignored; By died a broken man.

His work is still considered a marvel today. When completed, the canal covered two hundred and two kilometres and included forty-seven locks, twenty-four lock stations, four military blockhouses, and a handful of defensible lockmasters' quarters.

The impact was immediate. Mills, villages, and industries sprang up along the way as the canal became as important to the economy as it was to the military.

That heyday, though, would be short-lived. By 1850 the threat from the United States had waned, the St. Lawrence River was vastly improved for shipping, and the arrival of the railway was on the horizon.

Ironically, those early railways ultimately helped boost the use of the canal, as they brought increasing numbers of American fishers and tourists to the lodges and hotels that had begun to spring up. Recreational boating boomed in the ensuing years as well.

Despite its increasing popularity, the canal faced a few challenges. In 1932 the federal government gave serious thought to actually filling in the canal, but, happily, environmental concerns killed that idea. Then in 1966 the feds again had another brilliant idea: to electrify all the hand-operated locks, thus nullifying the canal's living heritage and negating any future UNESCO recognition.

Fortunately, the canal's heritage enthusiasts would have none of that. Led by Don Warren of Chaffey's Locks and other prominent individuals, the modernization was stopped, but not before three of the lock stations had their heritage replaced by modernization: namely Newboro, Black Rapids, and Smiths Falls. The forty-four remaining locks still require the ancient art of cranking open the massive gates by hand and include a pair of swing bridges, making the Rideau unique among the world's operating canals.

Its eastern terminus in Ottawa features the eight-flight locks that descend steeply down the limestone escarpment in the shadow of the Château Laurier Hotel into the Ottawa River. At thirty-five metres, it is the steepest drop in the system. The smallest drop,

by contrast, is at Kilmarnock, where the drop is less than a metre.

Most of the canal's heritage is within reach of local roads as they trace the banks of the canal from Hogs Back lock near Ottawa to Merrickville. From Smiths Falls, Highway 15, the Rideau Heritage Route, leads west to Newboro and then south to Highway 401 a short distance east of Kingston.

From Ottawa, the canal uses the Rideau River as its waterway. Among the many sites worth a visit is Watson's Mill at Manotick. Built in 1860 by Moss Kent Dickinson using local limestone, it was acquired by Aleck Spratt in 1927, who operated it until Henry Watson took it over in 1946. In 1972 Watson sold it to the Rideau Valley Conservation Authority, which has retained its water power function and opens it to the public for tours and events. Historic homes and one-time stores line the streets near the mill, including the Dickinson House, home of the original builder.

The Rideau Canal then passes through historic communities like Burritts Rapids, which dates from 1783 and predates the arrival of the canal itself. Such is the case as well with Merrickville, which dates from 1794, when William Merrick built a dam across the river to power his grist, saw, and carding mills. Merrickville became the largest centre on the canal between Ottawa and Kingston. Today it boasts a historic complex overlooking the locks that includes a large stone blockhouse, which contains a museum and is a National Historic Site, as well as Merrick's grand mansion and the ruins of his mills. The town's main street is lined with many stone shops leading to the three-storey Jacques Block by the lock station (now the Baldachin Inn).

Smiths Falls became more of a railway hub than a canal centre, although the Rideau Canal Visitor Centre is in the town. In 1859 the first tracks arrived from Brockville and were later absorbed into the vast CPR network. In 1885 the CPR opened a major rail yard, which still functions today. Another railway came to town in 1914, namely the Canadian Northern Railway. Although its tracks are now gone, its historic station is the focus for the Railway Museum of Eastern Ontario. At Slys Lock stands the 1862 mill keeper's house, which contains a collection of historic artifacts and an unusual two-storey outhouse.

West of Smiths Falls, the Tay Canal, a side canal, leads from the Rideau to the town of Perth, labelled Ontario's prettiest town. With its preserved main street of stone buildings, historic homes, and the park-like setting of the turning basin, no one will argue. Highway 43 leads from Highway 15 to Perth.

From Smiths Falls, Highway 15 takes over as the main road access to the canal's many historic features.

Here, too, the canal enters the waters of the Rideau Lakes. These waters serve as the headwaters for the Rideau Canal, with the locks leading downstream in both directions to Ottawa in the east and Kingston to the south. On the western end of Big Rideau Lake, the scenic village of Westport has become a popular day-use destination.

This, too, is where the canal leaves the Rideau Lakes through the lock station at Newboro. With its military blockhouse, it is the highest point on the Rideau system. From here it is downhill all the way to Kingston as it follows a chain of small lakes known as the "drowned lands." By needed to raise the water levels in these lakes and swamps to accommodate the canal's boat traffic. The swamps helped create malarial infestation, which took the lives of hundreds of canal workers.

From Newboro, Highway 15 leads south and offers signed access to the canal's many locks and historic features.

Among the most prominent is Jones Falls. Besides its three flight locks, the massive stone arch dam was considered an engineering marvel in its day, and at 20 metres high and 120 metres wide, it was the largest such structure in North America. Here, too, are the lockmaster's defensive quarters with their gun slits in the walls, a former blacksmith shop, and the triple locks, all connected with wooded walking trails. At the base of the locks, the Hotel Kenney, built in 1888 and one of the oldest on the waterway, still provides accommodation for guests and offers an elegant restaurant as well.

Chaffey's Locks contains a museum in the lockmaster's house, while the historic Opinicon Resort, built in the 1870s as a private residence and later expanded to become a lodge for fishers, offers comfortable accommodation, fine dining, and a popular ice cream bar.

Bedford Mills, a one-time milling and shipbuilding hub, has become a ghost town on a side channel of the canal. A powerhouse, restored mill, and wooden church are all that remain of this once-busy spot.

A number of other locks continue the descent to Kingston Mills. With its historic blockhouse, it is the last lock before the canal enters the Cataraqui marsh and Lake Ontario.

The Jones Falls Lock Station is one of the many marvels of early engineering on the Rideau Canal.

Bookending the canal with Ottawa is Ontario's "stone city" of Kingston, where its fortifications, built to defend the canal, form the southern terminus of the Rideau Canal and part of the UNESCO Rideau Canal and Kingston Fortifications World Heritage Site.

KINGSTON FORTIFICATIONS

Kingston's strategic military position has been valued since the time of the attacks by the Haudenosaunee on the early French settlements. To defend against the raids, in 1673 Count Frontenac ordered the construction of a wooden palisade where the Cataraqui River flowed into Lake Ontario just at its outlet into the St. Lawrence River. It was later replaced by the sturdier Fort Frontenac.

In 1753 it was captured by the British and demolished. The stone foundations of this early fort are today exposed in downtown Kingston. A more recent military establishment now houses the Tête-de-Pont military barracks.

With the outbreak of the War of 1812, the British built another fort on a high promontory on the opposite shore of the bay and called it Fort Henry. In 1832 the need to protect the entrance to the newly completed Rideau Canal meant that a more substantial structure was built, and a solid stone fort appeared in place of the earlier fort.

To complement the fort, a string of round stone towers, known as Martello towers, was built along the shore. These were an effective defence against

naval bombardment until exploding shells replaced the round iron cannon balls.

After the 1890s the fortifications sat largely unused until, in 1936, a Depression-era work project restored the fort. Following its use as a prisoner-of-war camp during the Second World War (escape attempts included crawling through a disused sewer system and hiding in a grand piano — both failed), it became a popular tourist attraction complete with military drills and concerts. The popular Sunset Ceremony each Wednesday includes mock battles and cannon fire, while tours take in the actual military facilities, including barracks, mess hall, and lock-up. Meals are available on the two-hundred-seat Battery Bistro Patio. Kids can dress in military uniforms before heading into the gift shop.

Of the little round forts, the Shoal Tower and the Murney Tower are both National Historic Sites; the latter also functions as a museum.

Meanwhile, on a peninsula between Fort Henry and the site of Fort Frontenac, the British established a naval depot known as Fort Frederick. In 1874 the site became the Royal Military College, one of North America's most prestigious military schools. On the site stands a structure known as the Stone Frigate, which dates from the fort's first days as a naval yard. Many of the additional structures date from the college's early days.

Although much of the greater Kingston area suffers from the usual urban sprawl, the core area retains many historic stone buildings, thanks again to the canal builders, including soaring church steeples, stone stores, and the magnificent 1840s domed city hall, originally intended as Canada's seat of government.

One of Kingston's Martello towers forms part of the Rideau Canal and Kingston Fortifications World Heritage Site.

THE TRENT-SEVERN WATERWAY

The Rideau Canal forms part of a longer canal system, the Trent-Severn Waterway, which links Lake Ontario from Trenton, a point west of Kingston, to Georgian Bay. Although this section of the route is not part of the UNESCO designation, it does offer some unique engineering marvels of its own.

The Trent portion began in 1833 in Bobcaygeon to help the lumber industry float its logs more easily from the forested highlands farther north to the mills. As part of the construction, the many Kawartha Lakes were dammed to eliminate the shallows and rapids that linked them.

Nine decades would then pass before the stop-and-start canal system finally linked Lake Ontario with Georgian Bay. This included a "ghost" canal built between 1907 and 1912 as a political ploy to link Newmarket, north of Toronto, with Lake Simcoe. Because the watershed contained insufficient flow, the canal never opened, and its ruins still linger to this day.

As construction of the Trent Canal crept along, a political decision was made to install lift locks between Lake Ontario and Lake Simcoe. These unusual locks consist of a pair of tubs, side by side, large enough to carry boats, which are connected by a valve that runs between them. While one tub, or caisson, rests at the top of the structure, the other remains at the bottom.

No external power is needed; the lift lock functions by gravity alone, using a counterweight principle. One caisson always ascends and the other always descends during each locking cycle. When one caisson reaches the top position, it stops thirty centimetres below the water level of the upper reach, and the control valve is closed. This creates a differential in the two weights, which allows the lifts to rise and fall. In Peterborough, the caissons measure forty-three metres long, ten metres wide, and more than two metres deep and can raise their cargo more than twenty metres in the air.

In 1979 the National Historic Sites and Monuments Board of Canada declared the Peterborough lift lock a National Historical Site and installed a visitor centre. Boat tours of the lock originate in Peterborough throughout the tourist season. In 1987 the American Society of Mechanical Engineers named the Peterborough lift lock a Historical Engineering Marvel Landmark.

A similar lock is located in Kirkfield, a short distance west of Peterborough, with a more modest drop of fourteen metres. Both locks were opened in 1907 and are the only examples of this type of lock structure in North America.

Yet another engineering oddity marks the Severn portion of the canal near its entrance into Georgian Bay. Again, the only one of its kind in North America, the Big Chute Marine Railway was devised to complete the Trent-Severn Canal link between Lake Simcoe and Georgian Bay.

The first version of the marine railway was completed in 1917, along with a similar system at the Swift Rapids in 1919, but was limited to carrying vessels only eleven metres long. In 1923 it was enlarged to accommodate boats up to eighteen metres long. In 1964 the railway at the Swift was replaced with a single lock, while a similar proposal was considered for the Big Chute.

However, the discovery of the sea lamprey in the Gloucester Pool below the chute meant that the railway remained the only way to prevent the migration of this deadly predator into Lake Simcoe. In 1978 the present railway was completed and now allows for vessels up to thirty-three metres long.

Controlled from a central tower using a system of cables, the operation consists of floating the boats onto the carriage, which is submerged into the water above the falls. The carriage is then lowered along the rails down the cliff and into the waters below, where the boats simply float off. The original carriage rests on display beside the original control tower.

TWENTY-FOUR

BRIDGING THE GAP:
CANADA'S ENGINEERING MARVELS

Canada is a country defined by geography. Her vast spaces, from the Carolinian south to the frozen north, her waterways, and her jagged mountains have determined Indigenous travel routes and European settlement patterns and have prompted feats of world-famous engineering.

For generations, geography ruled. Rivers and lakes provided highways and sources of food for their Indigenous inhabitants. Then, as the European invasion proceeded and the industrial age dawned, gaps in transportation presented formidable engineering challenges. Engineers designed early wooden truss bridges to cross streams and small rivers, while wider crossings used horse-powered ferries.

The advancement of railways and roads, however, tested the ingenuity of the engineers. Stone arch bridges led to longer truss bridges, suspension bridges, and cantilever bridges. And Canadian engineers were more than up to the task. Today, Canada has achieved world-renowned bridge-building feats and has built some unusual tunnels as well.

Wooden covered bridges, among Canada's earliest, have become an icon of the snowy regions of northeastern North America, in particular New Brunswick and Quebec.

Many create picture-postcard images with their rustic roofs and streams rushing below. Few, however, were anything like New Brunswick's Hartland Bridge. Completed in 1901 and spanning the Saint John River in New Brunswick, the bridge replaced an aging ferry and, at 391 metres, became the world's longest covered bridge.

The original design lacked the famous roof and suffered a number of closures. In 1907 a fire destroyed the central section, and in 1920 the middle portion collapsed into the river. The collapse prompted the addition of the peaked roof and wooden walls. In 1966 vandals tried to burn the aging structure, while trucks were barred from using it entirely in 1970. In 1980 the government of Canada designated it a National Historic Site. It has since survived a damaged post and split beam to remain the world's longest covered bridge.

The east coast seems to have become famous for having the longest bridges. And not all of them are old, as attested by the new Confederation Bridge, which spans the Northumberland Strait between New Brunswick and Prince Edward Island.

This multi-span modernistic structure is 12.9 kilometres long, the world's longest bridge over ice-covered waters, as the strait is for much of the frigid winters. At its highest it rises to sixty metres above the water to allow large vessels to pass beneath.

First considered as early as the 1870s, the idea of building a fixed link wasn't seriously discussed until the 1950s and 1960s. In 1873 Prince Edward Island's condition of admission to the new Canadian Confederation required that the federal government establish a navigational link for the new Intercolonial Railway, and two ferry services entered operation to the island from Pictou, Nova Scotia, and Shediac, New Brunswick. However, the original ice-breaking vessels were unreliable and seasonal, and in 1915 the government put a dedicated railcar ferry into operation followed by a car ferry in 1938.

Interest in a bridge resurfaced in 1957 when the Canso Causeway linking mainland Nova Scotia with Cape Breton Island opened. The first proposals called for a system of causeways and tunnels. However, the navigational gap would have forced ocean currents to funnel through at eighteen knots, or thirty-three kilometres per hour, an impossibility for ships to navigate.

The election of Brian Mulroney and his Conservative government in 1986 led to the abandonment of the island railway, along with the fixation of the Mulroney Tories on regional mega-projects, and brought the fixed link back to the front burner. Bitter controversy followed, but in 1992 the bridge received its go-ahead.

As construction proceeded, many names were proffered for the new link, including the Bidwell Bridge, reflecting the original Mi'kmaq name for the area. The name "Confederation" was ultimately selected because, in May 1997 when the bridge opened, the promises of Confederation made more than a hundred years earlier were finally fulfilled.

Today a private consortium operates the bridge and charges a toll for all vehicles, while a shuttle bus is offered to pedestrians and cyclists.

The Bill Thorpe Walking Bridge in Fredericton, New Brunswick, is reputedly the world's longest walking bridge. Built in 1886 as a railway bridge to link Fredericton with South Devon on the opposite side of the Saint John River, this truss bridge extends for 581 metres and was closed to rail traffic in 1996.

The Salmon River railway trestle near Grand Falls, New Brunswick, is listed as the longest trestle bridge in Canada. This sixteen-span structure stretches for four kilometres across the Salmon River and was erected in 1914 by the government's own National Transcontinental Railway. CN freight trains use the daunting bridge to this day.

Downstream from the world-famous historic walled city of Quebec, the mighty St. Lawrence is simply too wide for a bridge. However, where the river narrows between Quebec City and its counterpart on the river's south shore, Lévis, the location was well suited for the Quebec Bridge.

Such a bridge was envisioned as early as 1852. However, political dithering and instability delayed approval until the election of Wilfred Laurier's Liberals in 1896. Financial arrangements remained a hurdle until they were resolved in 1903, and construction began the following year.

Sadly, tragedy was close at hand.

One of the world's longest bridges and the highest over waters that freeze, the Confederation Bridge provides a road link between Canada's mainland and Prince Edward Island.

In 1907, as completion neared, chief engineer Norman McClure realized that the bridge structure could not sustain its own weight. However, before the bridge company was able to act, the structure collapsed, taking with it the lives of seventy-five workers, including thirty-three of the acclaimed Kanien'keha:ka high-rise steel workers from Kahnawake, Quebec. A royal commission subsequently determined that the fault lay with the bridge's design.

Then, even as reconstruction was under way, tragedy struck again, this time in 1916 when the central portion crumbled into the river, killing thirteen workers. Fault this time lay with the engineer responsible for that portion of the bridge.

In 1917 the bridge finally opened, mainly for the use of the National Transcontinental Railway, later to become part of the CN Rail network. At 549 metres, the centre span remains the world's largest cantilever structure. In 1996 the National Historic Sites and Monuments Board designated it as a National Historic Site.

Even that, however, hasn't helped to guarantee its survival. After the government of Canada transferred the ownership of the CNR to the private sector in the 1990s, the new railway owners showed little interest in the bridge's maintenance. By 2015, according to Heritage Canada, it had become one of Canada's most endangered historic sites, with 60 percent of the structure then covered in corrosive rust. Ultimately, the government took over responsibility for repainting the giant structure with help from the province.

Today the 987-metre-long bridge carries vehicular and pedestrian traffic while continuing its role carrying both freight and passenger rail traffic.

The name "Victoria Tube" does not refer to any London tube or subway system. Rather, it was the type of bridge, the first of its kind and at three kilometres long the largest in North America, to link the south shore of the St. Lawrence River to the booming city of Montreal.

When the Grand Trunk Railway began surveying its route in the 1850s, those tracks followed the south shore of the river. Anxious for a way to access the city, the railway could not rely on the existing ferry service, which was both limited and seasonal.

In 1854 the barges began to arrive with the steel beams for a massive new railway bridge project. Seventy-two barges were used to haul the material, while more than three thousand men (and children) set to work laying the piers and erecting the steel supports. Iron sections, prefabricated in Britain, were used to create the tube, which was essentially a fully enclosed tubular bridge. Its twenty-four piers were specially designed to break up the ice that flowed down the river and have since remained largely unaltered.

When the first trains began to cross in 1859, it was the world's longest bridge and hailed as the "eighth wonder of the world." But the trapped fumes from the steam engines inside the tube made for unpleasant and even dangerous conditions for those on the trains, and so the coverings were removed. In 1909 a second track was added to the north side of the bridge to accommodate a radial line, and in 1927 a vehicular lane was added to the south side. When the radial service ended in 1955, the bridge became a four-lane multi-use structure.

The only other major alteration was the creation of a second approach on the east end to accommodate the ocean vessels using the newly opened St. Lawrence Seaway.

To this day it has retained its original function as CN's main line to the Atlantic as well as carrying VIA Rail passenger trains to Quebec City and Halifax. Weight limits restrict the size of the buses that can use it, and large trucks are prohibited altogether. Traffic flows themselves are regulated so as to accommodate the direction of rush-hour volumes.

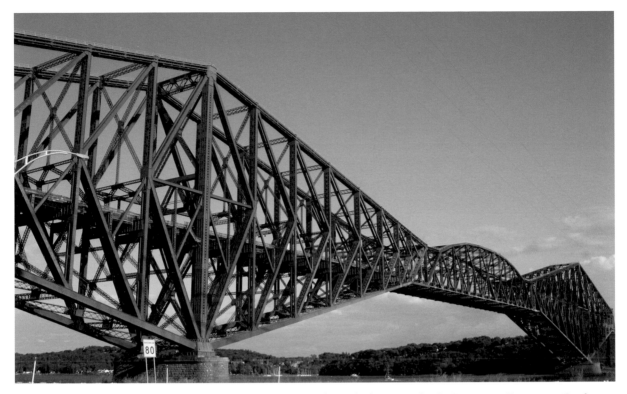

One of the world's largest railway bridges is the Quebec Bridge, which crosses the St. Lawrence River near Quebec City. It was the site of the tragic deaths of workers while they struggled to complete the massive structure.

The Montreal urban area encompasses many islands and river channels and can therefore boast many historic bridges, all of which display impressive engineering skills.

While the province of Ontario lacks the challenges of wide river crossings, it nonetheless offers several one-of-a-kind bridge structures. In Ottawa, a pair of one-time railway bridges was built to cross the Ottawa River. Completed in 1901 to carry the CPR over the Ottawa River, at the time, the Royal Alexandra, or Interprovincial Bridge, boasted the longest cantilevered centre span in North America. Its total length is more than 587 metres, and today, under the gaze of Parliament Hill, it carries vehicle and bicycle traffic only.

A short distance upstream, the CPR's Prince of Wales Bridge crosses the river in two sections split by Lemieux Island. Tracks remain in place while a decision on its future is pending.

Crossing Ontario's Mississippi River at Pakenham, although only eighty-five metres long, is the continent's longest stone arch bridge. With its five spans, it continues to carry vehicular traffic. It was completed in 1903.

Although only sixty-five metres long, the Blackfriars Bridge in London, Ontario, is described as one of the rarest and oldest bridges in Canada and a rare survivor on the continent. It incorporates an unusual delicate steel bowstring truss technique, a design that has limited weight capacity and therefore was rarely constructed elsewhere. Built in 1875 to cross the North Thames River, it carries only pedestrian and cycle traffic today and is designated as a provincial heritage site.

In the 1930s, in order to gain access to the country's growing road network, a wooden truss bridge was constructed across the Sioux Narrows between Rainy River and Kenora. When completed in 1936, at sixty-four metres, it was the world's longest single-span wooden bridge and was later designated as a provincial heritage structure. Unfortunately, deteriorating structural conditions required that it be replaced with a steel structure. However, in order to retain at least part of its heritage features, the steel frame was clad with wood from the earlier bridge. It lies on Highway 71 between Highway 11 and Highway 17 and is a Trans-Canada Highway alternative route.

Canada contains the world's largest freshwater island, Manitoulin, but no highway was ever built to link it with mainland Ontario. Rather, the only two accesses are by means of a car ferry, the MS *Chi-Cheemaun*, and an ancient railway swing bridge. The structure was built by the Algoma Eastern Railway and opened in 1913, carrying CPR rail traffic to the town of Little Current until the 1980s. As early as 1946 it was modified to carry vehicular traffic as well.

Today the tracks are gone. The bridge swings open for fifteen minutes each hour during the navigation season to allow vessels to travel the popular North Channel between Manitoulin and the mainland. Designated a provincial heritage site, it also serves as the island's icon.

With their flat prairie fields and rolling grasslands, Canada's Prairie provinces seem unlikely to harbour world-famous bridges. Yet, it is here that the world's largest railway structure of its type carries CPR rail traffic across the Oldman River at Lethbridge, Alberta. It was completed in 1909 to bypass a more circuitous rail route on the CPR's southern main line from eastern Canada to the Pacific Ocean. More than 1,600 metres long, this delicate-looking trestle rises thirty-three metres above the valley below.

Between the prairies and the Pacific coast, several ranges of rugged mountains provided a daunting challenge for railway construction engineers. While roads could simply wind their way along the valleys and over the mountain passes, railways, which had to maintain reasonably level gradients, enjoyed no such advantage and had to cross deep gorges and even blast through the mountains themselves.

Not surprisingly, throughout the mountains of western Alberta and much of British Columbia, the railways erected many stunning bridges. But it was the chief engineer for the Kettle Valley Railway (KVR), one Andrew McCulloch, who impressed the

Looming high above the Okanagan Valley, the Myra Canyon is a thousand-metre-high bowl-shaped canyon. Here, McCulloch carved his tracks into the mountain wall and used eighteen trestles to bridge the gullies and chasms along it. Following the end of rail travel in 1990, the right of way became a cycling and hiking trail, and, with the daunting Myra Canyon Trestles, it is one of the world's most desirable and challenging rail trails. Forest fires in the early 2000s destroyed many of the original structures; however, determined trail users and railway history lovers rebuilt them, and they are now a provincial heritage site.

As the mighty Fraser River flows into the Pacific Ocean where Vancouver now sprawls, it splits into a maze of channels. As in Montreal, the growing area soon needed several bridges.

Today the bridges that cross the Burrard Inlet between Vancouver and North Vancouver are among the world's most notable.

The best known is perhaps the Lions Gate Bridge, likely because Lionsgate is also the name of a major film production company. While the need for a bridge across the inlet was evident as early as 1890, it took until 1937 and two plebiscites before construction would start. One of Canada's most architecturally impressive bridges, the structure stretches more than 1,800 metres across the channel and rises more than 110 metres above the water. Increasing traffic congestion has necessitated many alterations and widening, including a reversible centre lane. Today it is a National Historic Site.

As urban growth sprawled unabated across the north shore of the inlet, it became clear that a second

A tricky trestle in the mountains of British Columbia.

engineering world with the feat that he accomplished and that even today is known as McCulloch's Wonder.

Opened in 1915, the KVR stretched for 260 kilometres between Midway near the B.C.-U.S. border and Hope on the CPR's main line. One of his best-known feats was the completion of the Myra Canyon Trestles.

bridge was needed. As the Lions Gate Bridge was built at the inlet's first narrows and known as the First Narrows Bridge, the new structure, at the next narrows, became the Second Narrows Bridge. The first bridge built at the second narrows was a combined rail/road bridge completed in 1926. Repeated collisions with ships led to its replacement in 1968 with a lift span to allow the large vessels to pass beneath.

By 1963 a new highway bridge was opened, and the railway bridge was closed to automobile traffic. The new highway bridge was finished in 1960 and today carries six lanes of traffic, removing pressure from the Lions Gate Bridge. But it came with a price.

While under construction in 1958, several spans collapsed, plunging seventy-nine workers into the water, nineteen of whom perished. In 1994 it was renamed the Ironworkers Memorial Second Narrows Crossing and became the subject of a country song by singer-songwriter Stompin' Tom Connors.

Sometimes, if the railways couldn't conquer their obstacles with bridges, they had to go through them. This has created some of the world's more interesting and unusual tunnels, perhaps none more so than the Spiral Tunnels of the Kicking Horse Pass.

In the 1880s, when laying their line through the Kicking Horse Pass, the most direct route through the Rockies, the CPR faced the challenge of a 4.5 percent gradient, a grade that necessitated extra engines be put on the trains being hauled through the gap. To conquer what was termed the "Big Hill," the CPR's design engineers proposed an unheard-of solution, a tunnel bored into the mountain in which the railway tracks circled around on themselves and emerged

seventeen metres higher than where they entered. The feat received worldwide acclaim and remains a popular roadside attraction even today. A viewpoint and interpretative signage lie 7.4 kilometres west of Field on the Trans-Canada Highway 1.

Another obstacle for the CPR was the Rogers Pass, where in 1890 a deadly avalanche killed seven workers and another in 1910 killed sixty-two. To avoid this deadly portion of the line, the CPR went into the mountains again and in 1916 blasted out the 8.5-kilometre Connaught Tunnel. Then, when the tunnel proved to be a bottleneck, the railway carved out yet another tunnel to allow for two-way train movement, the Mount Macdonald Tunnel. Opened in 1988, the 14.7-kilometre railway tunnel is North America's longest.

Following his engineering feat at the Myra Canyon, the KVR's design engineer, Andrew McCulloch, had another "wonder" up his sleeve. Near Hope, British Columbia, the hundred-metre-high cliffs of the winding Coquihalla River Gorge presented a near-impossible obstacle for the railway as the river twisted around the sheer granite cliffs. To build this section of line, the workers climbed down cliff ladders and were lowered in baskets hanging from the heights above. They blasted out a series of four tunnels, known as the Quintette Tunnels. The line opened in 1916.

Here, within a few hundred metres of each other, the tunnels were another of McCulloch's wonders, and today, with the tracks now gone, hikers and cyclists can gaze up at the sheer granite cliffs and marvel at McCulloch's accomplishment. Not too surprisingly, the spectacular canyon has attracted the moviemakers as dramatic locations at which to film such movies as *Shoot to Kill*, *Far from Home*, and *Rambo*.

Canada's West doesn't have sole ownership of Canada's most interesting tunnels. Another well-known tunnel still carries rail traffic beneath the Montreal landmark Mount Royal.

In 1912 the Canadian Northern Railway was looking for an entrance into downtown Montreal to compete with its rivals CPR and Grand Trunk Railway. However, Mount Royal stood in the way, so they blasted right through it. Opened a year later, the five-kilometre tunnel lies 188 metres beneath the summit of Mount Royal. Although the Canadian Northern Railway station no longer stands at its southern portal, electrified commuter trains still plunge through the tunnel to carry commuters to and from Montreal's northern suburbs.

A similar but little-known tunnel also plunges beneath the rocks of Quebec City. Excavated in 1930 to link the CPR's main line with its ocean terminal on the St. Lawrence River, the tunnel extends for 1.5 kilometres beneath the surface 110 metres overhead. With the opening of the St. Lawrence Seaway, the tunnel is no longer needed, although its two portals remain visible.

Canada's oldest railway tunnel lies beneath the Brockville city hall in eastern Ontario. Built between 1854 and 1860 for the Brockville and Ottawa Railway, the line connected the port at Brockville with Sand Point on the Ottawa River. The tunnel remained in use until 1970.

The tunnel has long been a tourist attraction, and the city has embarked on a project to open it for tourists from end to end. The existing tourist site at the southern portal, with its stone entrance, will link with the northern portal, which enters into a gorge near the existing CNR tracks. There the project envisions a roundhouse-style visitor centre, parking for motor coaches, and a trolley that will carry visitors to the southern portal and the waterfront. The tunnel extends 535 metres and lies 15 metres beneath the city.

While few original wooden railway trestles have managed to survive fires, rot, and replacement, the Kinsol Trestle, which crosses the Koksila River on Vancouver Island and was built in 1912 to link Nanaimo on the Esquimault and Nanaimo Railway with the logging town of Lake Cowichan, has done just that. At 44 metres high and 187 metres long, it is not just the highest wooden trestle in the Commonwealth, it is also one of the largest in the world. Abandoned in the 1950s, it now forms part of the TransCanada Trail, recently renamed the Great Trail.

TWENTY-FIVE

BLACK GOLD:
STILL PUMPING AFTER ALL THESE YEARS

No one travelling along Gum Bed Line near Oil Springs, Ontario, can avoid the odour and the pervasive creaking noise. The aroma is that of raw oil and the sound that of a system of "jerker rods" pumping oil as they have for more than a century.

To the surprise of some, North America's first commercial oil well did not spring into operation in Alberta or even Pennsylvania. That momentous event occurred in southwestern Ontario, southeast of present-day Sarnia.

Indigenous populations in the area had for generations used the black goo that seeped from the ground to caulk their canoes, but not for fuel. In 1854 Henry Tripp began extracting the substance from his property for use as asphalt. Then, in 1857, James Miller Williams acquired Tripp's property and began extracting the asphalt for commercial use. The following year, while digging a well for water, Williams struck oil at 15.5 metres and unleashed the world's first oil well. In 1858 he incorporated the Canadian Oil Company, the world's first oil company, to produce, refine, and market the product.

In 1862 a railway surveyor, John Henry Fairbank, purchased a parcel of land near the Williams site and discovered that his property also contained small deposits of oil. With the industrial revolution booming, oil was becoming an ever more valuable resource. In order to commercially extract the oil, which lay only a few metres below the surface, Fairbank devised a system of wooden rods that jerk back and forth across his fields, powered by a large cog in a nearby shack. The jerker rods operate a series of pumps that urge the black goo to the surface. This replaced the need for individual workers to hand-pump each well. To prevent the grass from interfering with the movement of the rods, a flock of sheep happily munched away as living lawn mowers and still do.

Additional deposits were found near Petrolia, and by 1864 the town of Petrolia could count seven refineries and the new town of Oil Springs twenty. But in 1866 plunging oil prices closed the small fields in Oil Springs, and Petrolia became the focus of production with refineries and related businesses. After the recession ended, a greater deposit of oil was discovered in 1881 in Oil Springs. More than a thousand oil wells sprang up as Oil Springs' population soared back up to three thousand, with nine hotels, several saloons, and a dozen general stores. The town became known as the oil capital of the world.

Oil fields at the location of the world's first commercial oil well at Oil Springs, Ontario, still operate with wooden jerker rods, a technology that is over a century old.

In 1862 another Petrolia oil man, Hugh Nixon Shaw, invented a drill that hammered through rock and till and unleashed Canada's first gusher, which blew a hundred metres in the air. Unfortunately, he had not devised a means to cap the flow, and Canada's first significant oil spill crept down a local creek and into the Great Lakes. Like a pile driver suspended from a wooden triangle, an example of his drill is on display at the Petrolia Discovery Oil Museum in Petrolia.

In 1873 Fairbank formed the Home Oil Company, and by 1880 it was Canada's leading oil producer. Meanwhile, oil drillers from Petrolia were earning a worldwide reputation for their expertise and were travelling as far away as the oil fields in the Middle East to apply their knowledge. Employing a distinctive pole-tool technique, they took their expertise and their reputation to places like Peru, Turkey, Russia, and Venezuela.

In 1896 Imperial Oil set up refineries in Petrolia, making it the centre of Canada's oil production for two decades. Following the First World War, however, new refineries opened in Sarnia, and those in both Petrolia and Oil Springs fell silent. Then, in 1936, a major oil discovery in the Turner Valley of Alberta revealed significant oil reserves in that province, and producers flocked to the new find.

A few decades later, in 1947, a new well burst into production near Leduc, Alberta, yielding an unheard-of 155 cubic metres a day. Production continued until 1974, after which the field was converted to gas production. Today the notorious oil sands of Fort McMurray have become Canada's leading extraction sites of oil.

A full-scale diorama of an early derrick operation.

No longer the centre of oil refining, Petrolia settled into a quieter existence, becoming a near ghost town. Many of the grand homes and main-street buildings, including the Victoria Opera House and turreted Grand Trunk railway station, still stand, making the town one of Ontario's best-preserved towns. The Petrolia Discovery Oil Museum is situated at the site of one of the town's early oil fields and includes displays of the early oil machinery. A short hiking trail through Bridgeview Conservation Area leads through the old oil fields themselves, where early artifacts can still be seen.

Meanwhile, back at Oil Springs, Fairbank's jerker rods still creak across the fields as they have with few modifications for a century and a half. Today his 350 wells yield twenty-four thousand barrels of crude a year. While it produces a mere fraction of that of the vast reserves of Alberta, the site now rates as a provincial heritage district and a National Historic Site.

From the Oil Springs Museum, the location of that first oil well, the Oil Springs Heritage Trail leads visitors past the heritage buildings in the village, which were built during the oil boom, and along the roads through the producing Fairbank fields themselves. Along the route, artist Murray Watson has created sixteen life-sized dioramas of the early methods of oil production.

The field has remained in the Fairbank family all that time and is now owned by John's great-grandson, Charles Fairbank, who has become a leading expert in the history of the Canadian oil industry. He is now a member of the Canadian Petroleum Hall of Fame.

In 2017 the county of Lambton, along with Fairbank, submitted an application to Parks Canada to add the Fairbank Fields and the Oil Springs Museum, to be called "Oil Springs Industrial Landscape," to its list of sites to be considered for inscription as a UNESCO World Heritage Site.

TWENTY-SIX

RIDING THE RAILS:
CANADA'S WORLD-RENOWNED TRAIN TRIPS

Railways have long been the historic life-blood of Canada. The earliest coal lines of the 1830s in Nova Scotia helped launch the industrial railway age in this country. When it became necessary to link the colonies with a more efficient transportation system than muddy roads and seasonal water routes, the Intercolonial and Grand Trunk Railways did the job and by 1857 were connecting Halifax, Nova Scotia, with Sarnia, Upper Canada.

Then, as a condition of British Columbia entering Confederation, the government of John A. Macdonald funded the construction of the Canadian Pacific Railway from Montreal to Vancouver. The Canadian Northern and the Grand Trunk Pacific Railways followed suit two decades later, and soon the country was criss-crossed with a spider's web of rail lines.

In eastern Canada, towns and villages vied fiercely to be included on the new rail lines, while in western Canada, towns were literally created by the new railways themselves on the land grants they received.

The Canadian Pacific Railway was the first to recognize the potential of the mountain scenery through which it passed. William Cornelius Van Horne, the company's general manager, famously proclaimed, "If we can't export the scenery, we shall import the tourists." And, by lobbying his friends in the Macdonald government to create a string of national parks on his route, he did just that. With its posters, postcards, and promotions, the CPR became one of the world's best-known scenic rail excursions.

Then, with the arrival of the auto age, the railway era began to fade. As early as the 1930s, travel by bus and personal car, and shipping by truck, was taking a toll on the railways. As rail traffic dwindled even further during the 1950s, rail passenger service was cut back and rail branch lines abandoned.

Air travel and highway construction accelerated the decline, and by the 1990s most rail passenger service had ended, while kilometre-long unit freight trains bypassed the local towns and villages.

Today, while rail travel is no longer the necessity it once was, it remains the most comfortable way to travel, thanks to the massive traffic congestion that clogs the highways of Canada's major urban areas and the discomfort of air travel. Today Canada is left with rail service that serves primarily only the larger urban corridors. Yet, the country retains some of the most scenic and popular rail experiences in the world.

The Rocky Mountaineer is a privately operated rail-tour company that offers world-renowned scenic rail trips in British Columbia, Alberta, and the U.S. state of Washington.

THE ROCKY MOUNTAINEER

This relative newcomer to the rail scene often tops the list of the world's best train rides.

The Rocky Mountaineer began as the name of a VIA Rail train. Launched in 1988, the train was intended to provide a scenic alternative to the Canadian, which travelled through much of Canada's wonderful mountain scenery during the night. VIA's Rocky Mountaineer train ran from Jasper to Vancouver with an overnight stop in Kamloops so that passengers could enjoy the mountains during daylight hours.

Sadly, the train lasted a mere two years; in 1990 the Conservative government of Brian Mulroney decided to cut VIA Rail's operations in half, and the Rocky Mountaineer was one of the victims. The brand was then sold to the Great Canadian Rail Tour Company, which became the Rocky Mountaineer.

The trains of the new Rocky Mountaineer rolled out of Vancouver's historic station in 1990 bound for Calgary with a tour called First Passage to the West, following the original route of the CPR's first western train. With an overnight stop in Kamloops, the journey offered its passengers daylight views of the spectacular peaks of the Rockies as well as the many ranges and canyons along the way.

The company has followed that with journeys with such names as Rainforest to Gold Rush, which follows the former route of the British Columbia Railway along the mountainous Pacific coast and into the mountains of Whistler and Pemberton, heading for the old gold rush town of Lillooet. From there it continues to an overnight stop in Quesnel before proceeding to Prince George and then Jasper. The Journey to the Clouds travels to Kamloops and then follows the Thompson River to Jasper.

The Rocky Mountaineer offers two levels of service. The Goldleaf service includes all-day use of a full-length dome car, gourmet breakfast and lunch, beverages, and an outdoor viewing platform. Hotels may include such luxury properties as the Fairmont Banff Springs, the Jasper Park Lodge, and the Palliser in Calgary.

The Silverleaf service includes travelling in a single-level dome coach with "regionally inspired" meals. Silverleaf hotels may include the Banff International Hotel or the Banff Park Lodge, the International Hotel in Calgary, or the Chateau Jasper, among others. Both levels include stays at the Chateau Lake Louise. Hotel stays in Vancouver may include the Fairmont Hotel Vancouver for the Goldleaf level, although a variety of properties in the city are possible.

Regardless of the level of service chosen, reviews are almost uniformly stellar. Travellers arrive from around the world to embark on the spectacular journey. Culturetrip.com rates the First Passage to the West trip as "one of the most scenic train rides in Canada, if not the world."

VIA RAIL'S CANADIAN

Close on the heels of the Rocky Mountaineer is VIA Rail's long-popular Canadian.

In 1955, in an effort to win back travellers who were fleeing the trains for their cars, the Canadian Pacific Railway launched the Canadian. Its sleek chrome coaches, with sleepers, domes, and the iconic bullet lounge bringing up the rear, gave its passengers a cross-country tour of Canada in luxury. Two separate sections, one from Montreal and the other from Toronto, joined up or split at Sudbury, depending on the direction.

The train was not just a luxurious way to cross the country; it also offered local coach service to the many towns and villages along its route, many of them in remote locations, travelling both night and day.

Making its way west from Sudbury, it would follow the cliff-lined shore of Lake Superior, one of the journey's most scenic segments. The most popular portion, naturally, was the mountains of the West, where it ventured through Banff and Kamloops on the way to Vancouver.

Like its popular sister train, the Canadian, VIA Rail's Skeena offers passengers stunning views of western Canada's mountain scenery.

Then, with lobbying from the CPR, the Mulroney government moved the route of the Canadian from the tracks of the CPR and onto those of the CNR, then a government-owned railway, now private. From Toronto — there is no longer a Montreal link — the route today journeys to Sudbury and then across northern Ontario. Emerging onto the prairies with a layover in Winnipeg, it continues on to Jasper, then along the canyons of the Thompson and Fraser Rivers before ending its four-day cross-country journey in Vancouver.

Although it no longer follows Lake Superior's cliff-lined shores, the less-scenic CN route does include attractive lake and river views. Unlike the Rocky Mountaineer, the Canadian travels through the night, omitting some of the wonderful mountain and prairie scenery on the way.

From Jasper, another VIA route, formerly known as the Skeena, travels west through the mountains of British Columbia and on to Prince Rupert. More geared to tourism, it travels only in daylight, offering an overnight stay in Prince George. Like the Canadian, it offers elegant meals and views from the dome, although sleepers are not necessary.

THE AGAWA CANYON

The Algoma Central Railway (ACR) was acquired by Sault Ste. Marie industrialist Frances Clergue in 1901 to haul logs and iron ore from his holdings in the northern Algoma region and, more specifically, his mines near the former gold rush town of Wawa

some two hundred kilometres north of Sault Ste. Marie. In 1909 he extended the line farther north to a junction with the CPR at Franz, the Canadian Northern Railway at Oba (both now virtual ghost towns), and the National Transcontinental Railway at Hearst.

By 1918 an artists' group, later known as the Group of Seven, had discovered the stunning beauty of Algoma's mountains and for the next five years would spend a week at a time in a rented boxcar outfitted to provide accommodation deep in the Agawa Canyon. Here, they ventured out to sketch the rugged beauty that appears on their many remarkable canvases, now so much in demand. Geologically, the canyon dates back 1.2 billion years, after which erosion and glaciation scraped out a fault line in the rock to create the canyon.

In the 1960s, realizing that the beauty of the canyon could bring tourists and revenue, the ACR began running day trains from Sault Ste. Marie to a stop in the canyon 183 kilometres to the north. By the 1970s and 1980s, more than a hundred thousand visitors a year were journeying on North America's longest passenger train, up to twenty-four cars long.

The Algoma Central is now owned by the passenger-averse CN Rail, which has threatened to end its local service to Hearst, thus eliminating access to the many remote lodges and cottages along the route.

Happily, the tour train that brings hundreds of jobs and millions of dollars in tourism revenue to the region still operates.

The day-long journey departs from a downtown station in Sault Ste. Marie and plunges northward, riding the crests of the many mountains before descending into Agawa Canyon over 150 metres below the summits.

After the train descends to the valley floor, passengers may enjoy a one-and-a-half-hour layover to picnic or climb three hundred steps to a stunning lookout point over the canyon, one of three trails in the park. The train offers GPS-triggered commentary in five languages as well as video screens that offer the passengers an engineer's perspective of the route.

Three-night packages in "the Soo" include visits to local museums, such as the Canadian Bushplane Heritage Centre, which recounts the stories and displays the aircraft of the pilots who risked their lives to carry people and supplies to Ontario's remote northern communities.

Canada's Lesser-Known Rail Adventures

Canada also offers a number of lesser-known scenic rail adventures. A regular VIA Rail train named the Abitibi departs Montreal three times a week to travel through Quebec's isolated northern regions, where many of the towns lie beyond road access, to the Abitibi region. The trip lasts the entire day, with returns usually the following day. Scenery includes the lakes and rivers of the Canadian Shield as well as the remote logging and trapping bush country beyond.

VIA's renowned Churchill train carries adventure seekers on a three-day excursion to polar bear country at the Arctic Ocean port of Churchill, Manitoba, as well as carrying local passengers to remote towns. The route was suspended in 2017 when floods washed out sections of the tracks.

Ontario's world-famous Polar Bear Express, while not venturing into polar bear country, does lead from Cochrane through the Hudson Bay lowlands, North America's largest wetland, to the remote Cree communities of Moosonee and Moose Factory, the latter the location of historic Hudson's Bay fur-trading buildings. The railway is operated by the Ontario Northland Railway.

In Quebec, a relatively new train operation is the Train de Charlevoix. This seasonal train runs between the stunning Montmorency Falls east of Quebec City and the town of Malbaie some 135 kilometres to the northeast. Its route carries it past the historic cathedral at Sainte-Anne-de-Beaupré and hugs the shore of the St. Lawrence River beneath looming cliffs. The train set consists of two self-propelled coaches with light lunches available.

Unfortunately, the federal government was not the only level of government to ignore the tourism potential of its railways and eliminate vital services. Another train service operated by the Ontario government's Ontario Northland Railway was known as the Northlander. That train, which ran daily from Toronto to Cochrane in far northeastern Ontario, offered its passengers an unrivalled cross-section of Ontario's history and geography as well as serving the citizens of the region.

In 2012 the provincial government cancelled the train on the pretext that it was not making enough money. However, the government had not promoted the service.

VINTAGE STEAM

Popular with Hollywood filmmakers are the various steam locomotive excursions in Canada. The oldest steam locomotives are those of the South Simcoe Steam Railway. Built in 1883 and used by the CPR, they pull vintage coaches along a short eight-kilometre track between Tottenham and Beeton. The brevity of the line is the result of objections by local politicians to extending the service farther and the short-sighted acquiescence of the Ontario government to allow the lifting of the rails. Still, the historic engines and coaches have provided the setting for several episodes of *Murdoch Mysteries* and PBS's *Shining Time Station*.

Volunteers in St. Jacobs, Ontario, have succeeded in restoring steam locomotive number 9, built in 1923, to operating condition, and the Waterloo Central Railway now runs steam excursions between north Waterloo and Elmira. It, too, has been

One of several railway steam operations in Canada, the South Simcoe Railway in Tottenham, Ontario, uses some of the country's oldest functioning steam locomotives.

frequently featured on *Murdoch Mysteries* and actively promotes its availability for film productions.

In Manitoba, the Prairie Dog Central operates a vintage steam locomotive along a route between Inkster and Grosse-Île northwest of Winnipeg. The 4-4-0 engine was built in Scotland in 1882. Albertans continue to enjoy the steam excursions of the Alberta Central Railway through the scenic prairie hills running between Stettler and the historic Canadian Northern Railway station in Big Valley. Visitors to the Okanagan Valley in British Columbia will have a chance to ride on the original track of the legendary Kettle Valley Railway in Summerville behind a 1929 2-8-0 steam locomotive named Spirit of Summerville.

The Alberni Valley Railway on Vancouver Island uses a 1929 2-8-2 steamer to operate the eight-kilometre route from Port Alberni's heritage railway station to the McLean steam-powered sawmill, which is a National Historic Site. The Kamloops Heritage Railway uses a 1912 2-8-0 steam engine along a short section of track that leads from Kamloops's heritage railway station, across the large bridge, over the South Thompson River, and along the banks of the scenic river.

A variety of heritage parks operate steam locomotives as part of the heritage experience. These include parks in Edmonton, Calgary, and Fort Steele and Duncan, both in British Columbia.

THE RAILWAY CASTLES

In addition to promoting their scenery to attract tourism, the railways also added to the landscape themselves with some of the world's most attractive railway hotels.

The most famous continues to be the Fairmont Banff Springs Hotel initiated by the CPR's Van Horne. Today the grand chateau-style structure, upgraded at the beginning of the nineteenth century and rebuilt in 1928 to replace the original after it burnt down in 1926, rises amid the mountains. It has long remained the iconic image of Canada's railway tourism, even though the CPR's trains no longer call.

The Grand Trunk Railway responded with the similar chateau-style Château Laurier Hotel, opened in 1912 and strategically located in the heart of Ottawa and directly across the Rideau Canal from the Canadian parliament buildings. Sadly, its main proponent, Charles Melville Hays, died on the *Titanic* before seeing its completion.

The most prominent landmark in Old Quebec is the Château Frontenac Fairmont Hotel, on which construction began in 1892. Again, repeating the grand chateau pattern of the CPR's hotels, it occupies a high promontory overlooking the St. Lawrence River and serves as a navigation guide for ships plying that river.

While not an older hotel, the Royal York Hotel across from Toronto's Union Station opened in 1929 and was, at the time, the British Empire's tallest building. It has hosted royalty, prominent world leaders, and celebrities from the entertainment world, including Frank Sinatra, Tony Bennett, and Olympic boxing champion Muhammad Ali.

While Europe and South Asia can rightly lay claim to having the world's most extravagantly built train stations, Canada's stations rank among the most classic in North America, with many of them echoing the railways' iconic chateau theme.

Among them, Quebec City's Gare du Palais, opened in 1912, reflects the classical rooflines of the old city and the Château Frontenac. Montreal's former Windsor Station, completed in 1889 in the Romanesque Revival style, was, according to the CPR's Van Horne, not one to moderate his words, "the best darn station in all of creation." It still stands. Toronto's classical Union Station with its row of pillars and Roman-style grand hall, opened in 1927 following two decades of the usual political dithering, is considered to be North America's finest station.

Two other heritage stations served as rare combination station/hotels. In downtown Montreal, the former Place Viger station displays the classic chateau-style rooflines that the CPR incorporated into its hotels. Today it is neither station nor hotel as it awaits new occupancy.

And in New Brunswick, in the tiny community of Macadam stands one of Canada's most stunning station/hotels. Built by the CPR in its classic chateau style, it opened in 1900 to serve as an overnight transfer point for well-heeled passengers making their way from the CPR's main line to Saint John and onto the branch line leading to the railway's St. Andrews by-the-Sea resort hotel, the Algonquin. The local community has restored the massive three-storey stone station, a National Historic Site with its own website, to its original elegance, while the CPR hotel in St. Andrews continues to attract vacationers to that scenic and historic seaside resort.

TWENTY-SEVEN

THE TRANS-CANADA HIGHWAY:
CANADA'S SECOND "NATIONAL DREAM"

When the first CPR trains puffed in to the Vancouver station in 1886, the railway was considered the new country's "national dream"; it linked the country not only physically but also politically. Then, eight decades later, another "national dream" was realized: the opening of the Trans-Canada Highway.

While the construction of the CPR took only a decade and a half, nearly six decades were needed to complete the highway link. At more than seven thousand kilometres, it is the world's longest named coast-to-coast highway. Mark Richardson, writing in *Maclean's* magazine, once described it as "a necklace across the country, linking Canadian provinces and their people to each other in a tangible, physical and highly visible way."

The kick-start for a cross-country highway predates even the First World War, when few Canadians had even seen a car. In May 1912 the car-loving members of the Victoria Car Club and the Canadian Highway Association gathered near the Pacific shore in Tofino, British Columbia, and pounded into the ground a sign that read "The Canada Highway." And so the notion of the Trans-Canada Highway was conceived. To encourage their dream, they offered a medal to the first brave soul to drive across the country using roads entirely within Canada. The problem was that there were none.

Nevertheless, a British journalist named Thomas Wilby, based in New York, believed that such an adventure would make a great story; he convinced the Reo Car Company to provide him with a vehicle and mechanic and off he went. (The Reo Car Company was named for Ransom E. Olds, who later lent his name to the Oldsmobile.)

On August 27, 1912, along with his mechanic and driver, Jack Haney of St. Catharines, Wilby dipped his tires into the Atlantic Ocean in Halifax. But the going proved to be rougher than he had expected. While he managed to make his way through Quebec and southern Ontario using existing roads, which were variously muddy and sandy, he discovered that in North Bay there was no longer any road at all. Against his wishes, he had little choice but to hoist his car onto a train and make his way to Sault Ste. Marie. Unfortunately, he missed the boat that would carry him to Port Arthur, where, when he finally arrived, he once more discovered that there was no road. So it was train again to the prairies.

Despite the gumbo roads, he managed to reach the Rockies. But here again he needed to resort to a combination of rail and rough mountain trails to bring him finally to Vancouver and then by boat to Victoria, where, on October 14, he could at last dip his tires into the Pacific. The medal was not to be his, however, for he had failed to remain on an all-road route.

Through the 1920s, Dr. Perry Doolittle continued to lobby on behalf of the Canadian Automobile Association for the road across Canada. And, indeed, in 1925 he drove across the country himself. Although he had better luck than Wilby, there was still no all-Canada road. Not until the make-work road building of the Depression years did the notion of the Trans-Canada Highway begin to resonate with the federal government.

By 1943 a crude road network did finally exist, and in 1946, Brigadier R.A. Macfarlane and Kenneth MacGillivray completed the first drive across the nation using all-Canadian roads, a feat they accomplished in just nine days. The medal was theirs.

The momentum for a national road had begun to accelerate. In 1949 the federal government passed the Act to Encourage and Assist the Construction of a Trans-Canada Highway — in short, the long-awaited Trans-Canada Highway Act. By upgrading existing provincial roads and adding new links, the TCH was intended to follow the shortest route between the oceans. Provincial lobbying, however, ultimately created a number of alternate routes.

There were to be strict construction standards. The road bed was to be between 6.7 and 7.3 metres wide, with a slope of no more than 6 percent and visibility no less than 183 metres. Provinces would build the road with the federal government shouldering 50 percent of the cost — 100 percent where the route passed through a national park. It would be completed by 1956. Or so they thought.

The inevitable federal-provincial disputes over jurisdiction and cost sharing delayed the opening until September 1962, when political dignitaries led by Prime Minister John Diefenbaker snipped the ribbon in the Rogers Pass in the Rocky Mountains.

The following year, Ed McCourt and his wife became the first to drive the new road (although they were to discover that much remained unpaved).

THE ROAD TODAY

The cross-Canada route today no longer presents the challenge that confronted Wilby, Doolittle, and MacGillivray. While there are those who hike it or bike it for charity, few car drivers undertake the journey as a must-do, which is somewhat unfortunate as the national highway provides a cross-section of our nation's history and geography as well as some of the country's most scenic and even oddest sights.

It almost seems like human nature to move from east to west. That, after all, is how the sun moves and how that first national dream unfolded.

While there is little opportunity to dip car tires in the Atlantic at St. John's, Newfoundland (which was not yet a part of Canada when Wilby started out), the boat launch at nearby Petty Harbour does allow that. But it will be from the Mile 0 marker in St. John's itself, with its iconic brightly painted cliffside houses and its historic Signal Hill, that the venture can truly begin.

Animal overpasses along the forested portions of the Trans-Canada Highway help reduce fatal collisions between motorists and wildlife.

While a long, dreary drive of seven hundred kilometres leads the Trans-Canada Highway (TCH) across the island province, many side trips lead along scenic peninsulas with their outports, coves, and intriguing place names, like Heart's Content, Heart's Delight, Tickle Cove, and the curiously named Dildo. (Dildo is a name that dates to 1711 and was a term often used for a nautical pin. Despite its modern sexual connotation, the town steadfastly refuses to change its name and, indeed, hosts an annual Dildo Days.)

Marine Atlantic's ferries connect Port aux Basques, Newfoundland, to North Sydney on Cape Breton

Island. It was at Louisbourg, a short distance east of North Sydney and site of today's wonderfully reconstructed and massive Fortress of Louisbourg, and not St. John's that trippers Macfarlane and MacGillivray dipped their wheels in the Atlantic for Canada's first all-Canadian cross-country road trip in 1946. (Newfoundland would join Confederation three years later.)

The Canso Causeway, built in 1955 to lure Nova Scotia to participate in the TCH project, connects Cape Breton Island with the mainland. From there, the TCH continues through the rolling Nova Scotia landscape to Moncton, New Brunswick. Rejecting that province's plea to route the highway through Saint John, the federal government instead took the highway through the capital, Fredericton, and then along the scenic shores of the Saint John River to Edmundston in the heart of Acadian country. Today the TCH has been widened and straightened, and now, as Highway 7, it bypasses the frequent riverside villages of its original alignment, including Hartland, with the world's longest covered bridge.

Once the TCH reaches the St. Lawrence River, it becomes Quebec Autoroute 20 and remains inland, avoiding the busier river road that was its original route. Up to Quebec City, the route displays scenic views over the wide river, passing several historic villages with their tall, silvery church steeples. After bypassing the ancient provincial capital that lies on the north side of the river, the TCH then moves farther inland along the flat and less scenic St. Lawrence lowlands.

Happily, today's TCH ignores its early route through the congested centre of Montreal and keeps well south of the city before crossing the St. Lawrence River farther west. Upon entering Ontario, it then swings northwest to follow the Ottawa River toward Ottawa. Here, it becomes Highway 417, again farther inland from its former alignment, the more historic and scenic Highway 17.

In Ottawa, the TCH becomes a major urban route and is frequently congested until it escapes the gridlock and enters the countryside of the Ottawa Valley as Highway 17. Passing outside the historic mill town of Renfrew, the TCH makes its way along the Ottawa River Valley and enters the rugged landscape of the Canadian Shield, where it encounters communities like Pembroke, Chalk River, and Deux-Rivières, with occasional views over the river to Quebec's Laurentian Mountains. At Mattawa, it veers west to North Bay and eventually to Sudbury.

Ontario ended up with more than one Trans-Canada Highway. An alternative route from Ottawa follows provincial Highways 7 and 12 west to Orillia, where it becomes Highway 69/400, and, after passing through the pink granite barrens of the Canadian Shield, eventually rejoins the main TCH at Sudbury.

This two-lane alternative is more varied than the main TCH 17, winding through a string of historic towns, such as Perth, known as Ontario's prettiest town, and Madoc, the jumping-off point for Ontario's first gold rush in 1866. (In that year, eager prospectors hurried to the supposedly fabulous gold find at Eldorado only to find many claims were fraudulent. Eldorado today is a virtual ghost town.) Marmora, the next heritage community, was once Canada's iron ore capital, remembered today with the historic Miner's Loop driving trail. Leading to Peterborough, TCH 7 encounters Hastings's historic mill and the unlikely railway town of Havelock. The city of Peterborough is the home of the distinctive Canadian Canoe Museum and Peterbororough Canal Lift Lock National Historic Site.

Beyond Orillia, the route merges onto Highways 400 and 69 north to Sudbury and the main TCH, 17. On the way, travellers can venture into the port town of Parry Sound and cruise the world-famous Thirty Thousand Islands and farther north visit the French River information centre to learn about the hardships of this ancient fur-trading route to the west.

Back on the Ottawa Valley section, after skirting the eastern boundary of Algonquin Park, the main TCH (Highway 17 here) swings away from the Ottawa River at the historic logging town of Mattawa and heads west to North Bay to meet up with another branch of the TCH, known as the truckers' Trans-Canada. Numbered as Highway 11, it is more level and, with fewer curves, is much favoured by long-distance truckers, although it is slightly longer than the original TCH. It leads north past historic mining towns like Cobalt and Kirkland Lake to the railway town of Cochrane and then west through Kapuskasing and Hearst before turning south to rejoin Highway 17 just east of the ill-fated Nipigon River bridge.

From Sudbury, the original TCH, Highway 17, continues west and passes what was once the Georgian Bay's most industrialized shoreline, with more than a dozen sawmill towns and a half-dozen early mining towns. The mills and mines are silent now, some having faded into ghost towns, while tourism now fuels the economic engine for the area.

This section also marks the start of the TCH's string of icons, beginning with the "big nickel" on Sudbury's outskirts to mark that city's ongoing role as one of the world's biggest nickel producers. North of Sault Ste. Marie (with its world-renowned Agawa Canyon tour train), the TCH encounters Wawa's famous giant goose, the third on the site and built to celebrate overcoming the highway's last gap. (The first goose failed to weather the elements and rests near a motel in town.)

The iconic Canada goose statue at Wawa, Ontario, symbolizes the point of completion for the Trans-Canada Highway.

The section of road between "the Soo" and this former iron-mining town was among the most difficult to build and, in 1966, was the last to be opened. The hills and lake vistas along the road between the Soo and Wawa mark the start of one of Canada's most scenic drives.

From Wawa (Anishinaabe for "wild goose" or "Land of the Big Goose"), the TCH cuts inland to the CPR divisional town of White River. It was on the platform of the White River railway station in 1914 that a Canadian army veterinarian, Captain Harry Colebourn, purchased a bear cub to be a mascot for his regiment, naming her Winnipeg after his hometown. In England, he donated the friendly cub, by then nicknamed Winnie, to the London Zoo. There a young boy named Christopher Robin Milne, whose favourite toy was a stuffed bear, became enamoured of the creature, inspiring his father, A.A. Milne, to create a series of children's books featuring an anthropomorphic character named Winnie-the-Pooh.

It is no surprise, then, that the town's newest roadside icon is a statue of the friendly little bear, having replaced the infamous thermometer that had proclaimed (incorrectly) that White River was the home of Canada's coldest temperature ever recorded.

Heading ever more westerly, passing rock outcrops and endless woodlands, the TCH comes to a more recent industrial area where Marathon, Terrace Bay, and Red Rock all emerged as smoky pulp mill towns in the 1950s. The 1980s marked a new gold rush to the Hemlo goldfields near Marathon, where the mines, most now depleted, retain their ghostly headframes by the road.

Here, too, the TCH reconnects with the cliff-lined Lake Superior shoreline, providing travellers with one of Canada's more scenic and world-renowned drives. It is an area that inspired Group of Seven artists such as Lawren Harris to create some of Canada's most iconic (and valuable) works of art.

This brings the TCH to the "famous" Nipigon bridge. A short distance east of the railway town of Nipigon, the two branches of the TCH, 11 and 17, join up again. Together they cross the canyon of the Nipigon River on a bridge that marks the only link between the road networks of eastern and western Canada. Any problem on this vital structure would sever the country's entire road network, which, in January 2016, is exactly what happened.

Following a prolonged but not unusual cold snap, the western end of the newly replaced two-lane span suddenly lurched sixty centimetres into the air, rendering the entire bridge impassible. All of Canada's cross-country traffic came to a sudden halt at the Nipigon River. Later investigation blamed the contractors for improperly tightened bolts, poorly designed shoe plates, and a lack of rotation in the bearings. The bridge's closure forced 1,300 trucks each day to endure a lengthy detour around the American south shore of Lake Superior, having to pass through two customs checkpoints. A temporary fix allowed the bridge to partially reopen a month later.

From Nipigon to Manitoba, the TCH becomes a tedious landscape of rock outcrops, boreal forest, and small lakes, interrupted only by the sprawling city of Thunder Bay and the foaming torrent of Kakabeka Falls. Interesting side trips, however, lead to the Sleeping Giant rock formation, a soaring limestone mesa that stabs into Lake Superior, and the ghost town of Silver Islet. Other ventures lead to Ontario's Grand Canyon, the Ouimet Canyon, and to the Panorama Amethyst mine, the last of the area's famous working amethyst mines.

There is another TCH icon here, and that is the monument to Terry Fox. Following the TCH for the most part, in 1980 this athlete, who had lost part of his right leg to cancer, ran a marathon a day to raise money for cancer research. The monument marks the site where recurring cancer forced him to end his

In 1980 Terry Fox, who had lost his leg to cancer, famously began a cross-Canada run, the Marathon of Hope, to raise money for cancer research. Terry's run came to a tragic end just outside of Thunder Bay when his cancer returned, forcing him to abandon his quest. Terry eventually succumbed to the disease, dying in June 1981. This monument in Thunder Bay was erected in his memory.

journey. He died the following year in Vancouver. He was just twenty-two. Over the following years, his courageous effort has resulted in the annual world-wide Terry Fox Run, which has raised millions of dollars for cancer research.

Northwest of Thunder Bay, Dryden marks the location of the infamous paper mill that leaked poisonous mercury into the English-Wabigoon River system in the 1960s and early 1970s, endangering the lives of the Indigenous Peoples that depend on its waters. It has yet to be completely cleaned up.

Eventually, the TCH makes its way into the Lake of the Woods tourist town of Kenora, once known as Rat Portage, with its own highway icon, a giant fish known as Husky the Muskie.

West of Kenora it is back to the landscape of endless rocks and trees until, just beyond the Manitoba border, the bushland thins and, like a curtain being drawn back, the flat prairie lands emerge. Here, the driver encounters the flat black soil, the blowing wheat fields, and that iconic prairie symbol, the grain elevator, some of which are visible for many kilometres. (Sadly, in the past two decades, more than 80 percent of these historic landmarks have been demolished as trucks replace the grain trains.)

Here, too, the road widens into four lanes and acquires the number 1. Although there is a TCH bypass (TCH 100) to what is often labelled Canada's most boring city, Winnipeg, the main route traverses the city and encounters the ambitious renovation project known as The Forks, which refers to the junction of the Red and Assiniboine Rivers. Here, in downtown Winnipeg, beneath the shadow of the city's grand railway station, several historic railway buildings have received new life as museums, markets, restaurants, and boutiques. Overlooking it all is the recently opened Canadian Museum for Human Rights.

Then it is off into the land where the railway companies literally created the towns, locating them every fifteen kilometres to allow trains to load up with grain at intervals convenient to the horse-drawn grain wagons. Alas, modernization of the railways and the grain industry have resulted in thousands of kilometres of abandoned rail lines, creating hundreds of little ghost towns.

While it is possible to bypass Portage la Prairie, a visit to the centre of town will lead to that community's two historic railway stations, situated right across the tracks from each other. That of the CPR is a handsome yellow brick structure that has become a museum, while that of the CNR may see the occasional visit of VIA Rail's gleaming TransCanada Canadian or its Arctic-bound Churchill train.

West of here, the TCH encounters another of its alternative routes, Highway 16, or the Yellowhead Highway, which angles to the northwest, passing through busy prairie communities like Yorkton and Saskatoon on the scenic South Saskatchewan River. Tracing the tracks of the Canadian Northern Railway, it passes through Edmonton and enters the Rocky Mountains before coming to Jasper. The rugged scenery follows the Yellowhead route to Prince George and Hazelton and ends at Prince Rupert on the Pacific coast.

As with the railway, the flat, treeless prairie allowed for speedy and easy highway construction. In fact, the main TCH closely follows the CPR main line to Regina, where the historic railway station has become a popular casino.

Farther along, the TCH enters into the city of Moose Jaw. This still-busy railway town was said to have been the Canadian headquarters for the infamous Chicago booze boss Al Capone. There was, after all, a direct rail link from Moose Jaw to Chicago. The town has capitalized on this dubious reputation by reopening a long-forgotten network of mysterious tunnels, supposedly conduits for the booze trade. In the revitalized downtown, the Capone's Hideaway theme motel displays a replica of a Capone-era car. Regrettably, the same revitalization led to a short-sighted municipal decision to demolish a string of Prohibition-era hotels for a new development. The history of an entire era thus fell to the bulldozers.

The TCH pulls clear of Moose Jaw and enters a landscape of rolling ranch lands. A short distance to the south, the ecologically rich Cypress Hills Interprovincial Park displays the grasslands that marked the home of their Indigenous inhabitants.

Near Brooks, Alberta, the remains of the unusual Brooks Aqueduct, a 3.2-kilometre-long raised concrete waterway, twenty metres above ground, recalls the efforts that the CPR undertook in 1910 to irrigate the vast, dry prairie that the railway had inherited. The waterway was closed in 1969 and is now a National Historic Site.

The next major city on the TCH is Calgary, home of the world-famous Calgary Stampede held each July. The city is also home to the remarkable Heritage Park Historical Village, which re-creates a nineteenth-century prairie town complete with a main street, relocated railway stations, and rides behind restored steam locomotives. Although the TCH passes through the north end of the city, a detour south on Centre Street to Eighth Avenue is worth the side trip. Here, several blocks of early commercial buildings have been preserved along a pedestrian boulevard. The nearby Glenbow Museum and Calgary Tower are worth a visit, as is the luxurious Palliser Hotel, the city's only remaining vestige of its railway roots.

As the TCH finally escapes Calgary's sprawl, the landscape changes dramatically. Looming ahead is the seemingly impenetrable wall of the craggy, snow-capped Rocky Mountains. The TCH enters the range along the valley of the Bow River, through the limestone ramparts, and arrives at Banff. What is now an overrun tourist destination began in the 1880s when the CPR's inveterate general manager, William Cornelius Van Horne, recognized the enormous value of promoting the site as a tourist destination. He prompted the federal government to create a national park and commenced construction of the spectacular Banff Springs Hotel (part of the Fairmont chain) with its chateau-style towers and rooflines that rise high above the valley of the Bow River.

A short distance west along Highway 1, another CPR hotel, the Chateau Lake Louise, attracts visitors by the busload to this scenic lakeside property surrounded by high mountain peaks. Happily, both Banff and Lake Louise have retained their CPR railway stations, a link to their respective railway roots. A more genuine TCH experience would be to follow Highway 1A between Banff and Lake Louise along the old highway's original alignment.

From Lake Louise, Highway 93 leads north from the TCH along the spectacular Icefields Parkway, designated by *National Geographic* as one of the world's most scenic roads.

Through the several ranges of mountains, there is no such thing as a straight line. The TCH continues to parallel the route of the CPR through one-time railway towns like Field and Golden before descending into Revelstoke, which still functions as a key railway town. Here, too, lies one of Canada's pre-eminent railway museums, the Revelstoke Railway Museum.

A short distance farther on, the TCH comes to one of Canada's most historic locations, Craigellachie, the site of the CPR's "last spike," where in 1885 a silver spike was driven into the rail line, symbolically uniting the country both physically and politically. The site is marked today with a cairn, an interpretative plaque, a caboose and railway-themed gift shop, and an information centre.

The route then makes its way out of the cloudy mountains and into the Okanagan Valley, Canada's driest region. Then it's back into mountain country as the route enters the deep canyons carved by the Thompson and Fraser Rivers. En route, the TCH passes above the foaming torrent known as Hell's Gate, where an aerial tramway gives brave visitors a bird's-eye view of the rushing waters.

Finally, the TCH makes a westerly lurch out of the mountains and into the Fraser River Delta and the sprawling suburbs that extend outward from Vancouver. After making its way through New Westminster and Burnaby, the TCH crosses the Burrard Inlet on the infamous Second Narrows Bridge (which killed nineteen men and injured twenty others when it collapsed during construction in June 1958).

From Horseshoe Bay north of Vancouver, B.C. Ferries carries TCH travellers across the Georgia Strait to Nanaimo, where the highway then leads southward into the provincial capital of Victoria and the western Mile 0 marker beside Beacon Hill Park.

However, to reach Tofino, the historic point where the original "Canada Highway" sign first appeared, it is necessary to return to Nanaimo and follow Highway 4 to Tofino, where a marker proclaims the place to be the true western terminus of the TCH. While correct in that Tofino marked the launch of the lobbying for a national highway, it was subsequently decided that the new road would be one that would link provincial capitals, thus the alignment from Nanaimo to Victoria rather than to Tofino, although, oddly, the final route bypassed other provincial capitals, such as Toronto, Edmonton, Halifax, and Quebec City.

Thus ends a genuine national adventure, one that crosses Canada's many landscapes and looks into historic locations. Unlike those early road warriors, today's traveller will find paved highways, modern accommodation, and interpretative signage. Yet, it can seem like a modern adventure revisiting the path of the country's first tire tracks.

(As a footnote, although it is not part of the TCH road network, in November 2017 a 138-kilometre all-season road opened through the Northwest Territories, linking Inuvik to Tuktoyaktuk on the Arctic Ocean, giving Canadians road access to all three ocean coasts.)

TWENTY-EIGHT

LA GASPÉSIE: QUEBEC'S LIGHTHOUSE TRAIL

It is one of Canada's lesser-known scenic routes, yet it ranks with the world's most rugged. For 270 kilometres, Quebec's Route 132 hugs the cliff-lined southern shores of the Gulf of St. Lawrence, passing through the picturesque villages of the Gaspé Peninsula tucked into protective coves, many of which are guarded by some of Canada's oldest and most historic lighthouses.

Beginning at Matane, about 409 kilometres northeast of Quebec City, it is often known as the Lighthouse Trail and encircles the Gaspé Peninsula, where ocean waves rush against rocky headlands.

The rugged peninsula is an extension of the Appalachian mountain system jutting into the Atlantic Ocean. At 31,075 square kilometres, the peninsula covers an area larger than the entire country of Belgium. With a population of more than 140,000, it is said to be the only region aside from the Channel Islands to retain the Norman Jersey dialect. The name Gaspé itself derives from the Mi'kmaq name *Gespeg*, meaning "land's end," a very fitting name.

At Matane, the route encounters what has been described as one of Canada's most outstanding horticultural attractions, the Jardins de Métis, also known as the Reford Gardens. This eighteen-hectare garden, one of the many National Historic Sites along this route, offers 1.6 kilometres of paths that lead through eighteen different themed gardens, such as the Blue Poppy Garden, the Bird Garden, and the Azalea Walk.

The garden was started in 1926 by Elsie Reford, on doctor's orders, a passion that she pursued until her death in 1954. The gardens form the grounds of the historic Estevan House, originally built for Sir George Stephen in 1887. The grounds were designated a National Historic Site of Canada in 1995 and are open to the public between May and October. A restaurant and café offer meals for those in need of nourishment.

As the route continues along the shore, the mountains begin to encroach on the road until they hug the road on one side, while waves crash on the other. The rocky uplands are part of the Chic-Choc mountain range and the Parc national de la Gaspésie.

The Cap-Chat lighthouse, seventy-one kilometres from Matane, offers accommodation in the former lightkeeper's house. At La Martre, forty-two kilometres from Cap-Chat, the distinctive bright red lighthouse containing the Musée des Phares (lighthouse museum) provides an interpretation of the heritage of these vital navigational aids.

The distinctive red La Martre Lighthouse on Quebec's Lighthouse Trail is now a historic attraction.

From here, the road continues to follow the mountainous peninsula in a northeasterly direction, occasionally entering into little coves that offered meager protection to what were once isolated fishing villages with names like Petite-Tourelle, Rivière-à-Claude, L'Anse-Pleureuse, and Gros-Morne.

At Rivière-la-Madeleine, sixty-nine kilometres from La Martre, the 1907 lighthouse rises twenty-nine metres above a cliff that itself looms forty-six metres above the crashing waves of the Atlantic. There has been a lighthouse here since 1871. Tours are available as well as a café in the former keeper's house.

Fifty kilometres farther takes Highway 132 to Grand-Étang, where a side road leads from the highway to the water's edge and the Renommée wooden lighthouse, another National Historic Site. This structure was returned here to its original site in 1997 after spending two decades in Quebec City.

From here, the peninsula bends to the southeast and leads through L'Anse-au-Griffon, now a virtual ghost town, where once a larger population worked at the various sawmills that turned out wood for barns, shingles, wharves, and piers. At fifty-five kilometres from Grand-Étang, the road leads to Canada's tallest lighthouse at Cap-des-Rosiers. Another National Historic Site, this 1858 lighthouse stands thirty-four metres high. Guided tours are available here as well.

Approaching the tip of the Gaspé Peninsula, Route 132 swings inland, crossing the tip of the peninsula to the shores of the Baie-des-Chaleurs and the entrance to the rugged coastline of the Forillon National Park. Here lurk the ghosts of the vanished fishing village of Grande-Grève, where hundreds of workers for two fishing companies salted cod for shipment to the West Indies and Europe.

Today only vague foundations remain, although two historic structures have been restored and are open to the public. These include the Hyman and Sons General Store, built originally in 1864 as a private home. It re-creates a general store of the period with costumed interpreters. The other is the Blanchette homestead.

From the parking lot at the end of the road, a trail leads to the lighthouse at Cap-Gaspé, perched high atop a dizzying ninety-five-metre cliff.

Route 132 then rounds the head of Baie de Gaspé and follows the south shore of the bay into the historic town of Gaspé, considered by many to be where "Canada" began. For it was on these shores that on July 24, 1534, while searching for a shortcut to the riches of the Far East, Jacques Cartier erected a cross and "claimed" the land for France. He did not appear to ask permission of the Indigenous Peoples.

Following Champlain's visit early in the following century, fishers from France began to seek out the protected coves of the Gaspé Peninsula, and the European invasion began. Gaspé's museum offers the history of the region along with a memorial to Cartier and a cross where he is said to have placed his cross.

Beyond Gaspé, Highway 132 still clings to the shore, but it is a much tamer shoreline here, with farms mixing with summer homes and chalets, until after sixty-two kilometres the road leaves the seaside and enters the ancient mountain range. As the road mounts the crest of a hill, it reveals an ocean vista that includes what many consider the climax of the route: the massive and much-photographed rock known as Percé.

Millions of years have passed since erosion separated this massive ship-like outlier from the mainland. Pounding waves wore into the limestone layers, carving out the two natural arches that gave the rock its name. One of the arches later collapsed, leaving a separate pillar beside it.

At low tide, a gravel bar leads to the base of the rock, although current safety concerns threaten to place this access off limits.

The rock's worldwide fame has turned Percé from a quiet fishing village into a sprawling tourist town with museums, motels, restaurants, and gift shops. Small tour boats will take visitors to the mighty rock and then continue on to circumnavigate Bonaventure Island.

Along with Percé Rock, the island was designated a National Migratory Bird Sanctuary in 1919,

Quebec's scenic Lighthouse Trail leads to the bird sanctuary of Bonaventure Island on the Gaspé Peninsula.

with more than fifty-three thousand pairs of nesting northern gannets situated in the crevices of the seventy-five-metre-high cliffs, along with common murres and black-legged kittiwakes.

Although Bonaventure's living cliffs are out of bounds to visitors, several trails lead around the 1,400-hectare island, where the remains of a one-time farming and fishing community yet lie. Both the island and the rock are also part of the provincial Parc national de l'Île-Bonaventure-et-du-Rocher-Percé.

From Percé, Route 132 makes its way along the Baie-des-Chaleurs, where it passes through a string of villages, some scenic, others not so much, and an endless string of summer homes. Early access along this shore was by the Quebec Atlantic and Oriental Railway, which had begun in 1907. A number of heritage train stations can still be found along the abandoned tracks, which, until a few years ago, was the route of VIA Rail's Chaleur train ride, one of Canada's most scenic routes. Lack of maintenance by CN Rail and by the subsequent owner, the Chemin de fer Baie des Chaleurs, however, has rendered the tracks unfit for train travel. The buses that replaced the trains were later cancelled as well.

Communities like Grande-Rivière and Bonaventure, which line the route, began as fishing settlements, while place names like New Carlisle and Richmond reflect the Anglophone roots of the region's early settlers. Perhaps the most scenic of the seaside villages is the fishing village of Port Daniel. Situated on the rocky shores, it still retains its attractive train station, which, like the others, has found a new lease on life.

At the head of the bay stands the community of Matapédia on the border with New Brunswick and situated about 334 kilometres from the village of Gaspé. The route then leaves the coastline for good and makes its way up the scenic Matapédia Valley and parallels the tracks of one of Canada's earliest railway lines, the Intercolonial Railway, passing communities like Amqui and Causapscal, both of which have retained their repurposed train stations. The tracks are still used by VIA Rail's Ocean Limited to Halifax.

Emerging from the Matapédia Valley at Mont-Joli, 140 kilometres from Matapédia, and sixty-three kilometres southwest of Matane, Highway 132 arrives back on the shores of the St. Lawrence, closing the circle on one of the world's most scenic oceanside drives.

TWENTY-NINE

CAPE BRETON'S WORLD-FAMOUS CABOT TRAIL

The famed travel and geography magazine *National Geographic* describes the Cabot Trail as "one of the most memorable drives in North America." It has also become one of the most popular in Canada.

Cape Breton, a 10,300-square-kilometre island, is separated from mainland Nova Scotia by the kilometre-and-a-half-wide Canso Strait. It has known human habitation with the Mi'kmaq First Nation for more than eight thousand years. Portuguese fishers began to arrive in the 1500s and established summer fishing colonies. Scottish highlanders began arriving in the late eighteenth century, expelled from their farms in Scotland and drawn by the resemblance of the rugged, windswept terrain to their own beloved home country.

The French had claimed the island as early as 1534 but largely ignored it. While the Treaty of Utrecht in 1713 marked the defeat of the French by the English, France retained the island, which they called Île Royale, and began building the remarkable Fortress of Louisbourg. Their occupation was short-lived, and the British regained possession in 1763.

By 1820 Britain had merged the colonies of Cape Breton and Nova Scotia, and shipbuilding had become the island's leading industry. When coal was discovered deep underground in northeastern Cape Breton, mining replaced shipbuilding as the mainstay of the island's economy, leading to the building of its first rail line linking the mines to the shipping ports of Louisbourg and Sydney.

However, the forbidding, barren, windswept plateau of the Cape Breton Highlands, which dominate the northwestern part of the island, remained little touched, except for small Acadian fishing settlements that sheltered in the coves along the cliff-lined west coast. These were settled by descendants of Acadian deportees who began to return following the French Revolution of 1789, their only link with each other and to the outside world being a perilous passage over open water.

After the French lost Île Royale to the British, the area around Ingonish became the focal point for Irish and Scottish arrivals. For the most part, however, Cape Breton's rugged northern highlands held less appeal for immigrants than did the friendlier terrain around the Bras D'Or Lakes and along the Margaree Valley. While fishers and farmers struggled, coal mining continued to prosper, despite horrific loss of life from mining explosions and collapses, which claimed 1,321 lives between 1866 and 1987.

To ease some of the travel difficulties of the cape's rugged western coastline, in 1932 the province opened a winding dirt road to link the little fishing settlements. Prior to that, only a crude trail linked the isolated coves, while the high plateau of North Mountain remained a barrier between two coasts.

With the dawn of the age of auto tourism, some of the hardier car enthusiasts began to brave the rugged cliffside roads to discover the dramatic beauty of the three-hundred-metre-high cliffs and the ocean waves that crashed into them. Four years later the government of Canada designated the Cape Breton Highlands as a national park, one of the first in eastern Canada.

The 950-square-kilometre park is comprised largely of a high, windy plateau into which two dozen rivers have carved deep valleys, a process that has taken millions of years. While 88 percent of the park is forested, portions of the highest reaches of North Mountain resemble Arctic tundra.

Not too surprisingly, the rugged beauty of this region began to attract wealthy American vacationers, such as rubber baron Henry Corson, who built his Keltic Lodge on the long peninsula known as Middle Head.

Meanwhile, Alexander Graham Bell, by now wealthy from his invention of the telephone and eighty-eight other patents, had already discovered the area and in 1893 built his summer home, which he called Beinn Bhreagh, on a hillside overlooking the Bras d'Or Lake.

Following the end of the Second World War, roads improved and auto tourism increased. Then, in 1955, the completion of the Canso Causeway finally gave Cape Breton Island its long-sought (or reviled, depending on the point of view) road link with the Nova Scotia mainland. The province began promoting the island, and especially the Cabot Trail, as a destination.

Since that early time, the Cabot Trail road has been widened and many of its more dangerous twists and turns straightened. Here, visitors may enjoy picturesque villages and vistas that take in wide valleys, soaring cliffs, and crashing waves. They will also discover a pride of heritage that has helped to preserve and celebrate ancient Gaelic and Acadian traditions long lost in most other parts of the world.

The ideal point to begin the scenic and historic Cabot Trail with its distinctive roadside markers is at Baddeck, situated on the Trans-Canada Highway on the shore of the Bras d'Or lakes, for this location marks the site of the excellent Alexander Graham Bell National Historic Site. Following his success and his fortunes from the telephone, Bell summered on the shore of the lakes and went on to invent many additional devices for which he assiduously and wisely took out patents, more than eighty-eight in total, although many of his inventions remained little known.

Others gained wide acclaim. While the Wright Brothers in the United States had completed the first manned flight at Kitty Hawk, Bell created Canada's first aircraft, which he named the Silver Dart. He then proceeded to create a hydrofoil, which set speed records in 1919, becoming the world's fastest boat. Other inventions include the metal detector and, surprising to many today, a wireless telephone, the precursor to the cellphone.

The museum displays many of his inventions (a behind-the-scenes tour known as the "white glove" tour reveals his many other contraptions and devices). On full display are replicas of his hydrofoil and an operating version of his Silver Dart aircraft.

Photos and mementos of his family history round out the amazing life of this remarkable inventor. Not on display, however, is his grand summer mansion, the stunning Beinn Bhreagh. Although it is now a designated heritage property, it remains with the family, who have not opened it to public viewing. Boat tours, however, will allow the curious to view it from the lake.

From Baddeck, the route follows the Trans-Canada Highway to exit 11 at St. Anns and the start of the trail's 298-kilometre scenic portion. Most seasoned travellers will advise following the trail in a counter-clockwise direction, as this will put the best scenic views and lookout points on the more convenient right-hand side of the vehicle.

St. Anns is the Gaelic heart of Cape Breton, where until recently many retained Gaelic as their home language. Here, the Colaisde na Gàidhlig, the Gaelic College of Celtic Arts and Crafts, teaches students traditional weaving, cuisine, music, and, most importantly, language, as well as the art of kilt making. Unique in North America, the college has been instrumental in preserving and celebrating the island's Gaelic heritage for nearly eighty years.

As the Cabot Trail twists over mountainous headlands and along the eastern shore, it offers lookouts and seaside vistas as it continues for seventy-three kilometres to the historic Ingonish Beach and the renowned Keltic Lodge resort.

Now a luxury resort and spa, the Keltic Lodge marks the site of Henry Corson's summer home. When the national park was designated in 1936, the provincial government purchased the property, now operated by Parks Canada, and offered rooms to the public. The resort closed temporarily during the Second World War (during which time it is said that German U-boat commanders would come ashore) and reopened in 1946.

With its booming popularity, the old buildings were replaced in 1952 with today's Tudor-style buildings. Today the lodge is a member of Historic Hotels Worldwide. The adjacent Highland Golf Course is ranked among Canada's top ten golfing experiences and is number sixty-six in the world. The property is located halfway along Middle Head, a narrow peninsula that splits Ingonish Bay in two, and looks across the waters to the 230-metre-high Cape Smokey to the east.

Ingonish also marks the eastern entrance to the national park. Here, too, lies the famous Ingonish Beach, a stretch of sand that *Canadian Geographic Traveller* ranks as among the top twenty-five beaches in Canada. From here, the visitor can continue north to Black Brook Beach and hike the Jack Pine Trail, a short and easy walk through a variety of forest ecosystems to the cliffs of the Atlantic. A longer eleven-kilometre scenic trail known as the Coastal Trail links Black Brook Beach with Neil's Harbour and connects with the Jack Pine Trail and the Jigging Cove Trail.

From Neil's Harbour, the Cabot Trail skirts Mica Mountain and comes to the former fishing communities of Aspy Bay. It was here in 1497 that John Cabot met the original Mi'kmaq inhabitants and opened the way for European fishers to establish summer fishing colonies. Protective harbours like Dingwall Harbour, South Harbour, and North Harbour still offer refuge to local fishing fleets, although tourism has become the main economic driver for the region.

From Aspy Bay, the trail leads up the scenic Aspy River valley, carved into a geological fault line within the massive North Mountain. Travellers may pause at the lookout point high up in the valley, while geologists would rather ponder the secrets of the past revealed in the rocky valley walls. Here, the ancient layers of gneiss and anorthosite date back more than one billion years.

From the head of the Aspy Valley, the Cabot Trail mounts a high plateau and over the divide, passing through terrain more typical of the Arctic tundra, with open barrens and stunted trees. The divide separates the Atlantic coast to the east from the Gulf of St. Lawrence on the west.

The route then descends the valley of the Grande Anse River and past the site of Lone Shieling, a re-creation of a Scottish crofter's dwelling and a glimpse into the life of the Highlands' earliest settlers. Here, too, in contrast to the bleak summits, are some of Canada's oldest maple trees.

At the coast, the community of Pleasant Bay, a sheltered cove for the early fishers, offers the Whale Interpretation Centre and tours into the gulf to seek out the many whale species that inhabit the waters. From here, another scenic road branches northward along the coast for eight kilometres to the monastery known as Gampo Abbey, where during the summer months tours are offered to visitors. From the clifftop of the abbey, the view extends across the wide gulf waters.

The main route of the Cabot Trail continues south from Pleasant Bay for forty-three kilometres to the distinctly Acadian community of Chéticamp. Along this portion, the trail winds up and down the steep coastal cliffs, revealing those dramatic and iconic vistas much publicized in tourist brochures and TV commercials.

Along this portion, after twisting its way up onto the high plateau, the trail reaches a lookout point with views down the valley to the vanished community of Fishing Cove, once a small but bustling settlement linked to the outside only by water.

The trail then continues along the Boar's Back and over MacKenzie Mountain, 355 metres above the waters below. Intrepid hikers may wish to venture onto the aptly named Skyline Trail, a three-hour hike to the summit of the three-hundred-metre-high cliffs overlooking the gulf.

As it winds back down to the water's edge, the Cabot Trail comes to the popular Cap-Rouge viewpoint with the Veteran's Monument. By the water, the rock formations at the La Bloc picnic site and Pillar Rock at Presqu'ile are where the crashing waves put on their best foamy display.

At this point, the Cabot Trail reaches the village of Petit Étang and the southern limits of the Cape Breton Highlands National Park. But the Cabot Trail is about more than spectacular ocean vistas, for here it also marks the beginning of the Acadian coast.

Acadian names like Petit Étang, La Prairie, and Belle-Marche provide evidence of the French

The breathtaking Skyline Trail is part of the Cabot Trail in Cape Breton Highlands National Park.

influence in the area, the focus of which is the seaside port of Chéticamp, where the one-time isolation of the region has helped maintain its Acadian roots and language.

Nowhere is this more notably celebrated than at the Mi-Carême Interpretive Centre located at Grand Étang, some eleven kilometres south of Chéticamp.

The Mi-Carême is an ancient Acadian celebration, representing a break from the restrictions of the Lenten season. During the week-long festivities, celebrants don elaborately painted face masks and venture from home to home, challenging the inhabitants to guess who they are. The centre displays the story of the festival as well as many of the elaborate masks and costumes that have been worn. Visitors may even be invited to create their own masks. A side benefit of the location is the little harbour that shelters the lobster boats that may arrive during the lobster season and offload their shelled catch for delivery to nearby markets and restaurants.

Another dozen kilometres leads to the larger fishing harbour of Margaree Harbour, where the wharfs bob with rows of lobster boats. Island Sunset Resort offers visitors a final glimpse of the Cabot Trail's coastal route.

From Margaree Harbour, the Cabot Trail swings inland to follow the picturesque and decidedly more fertile and gentle valley of the Margaree River and the Middle River, leading back to Baddeck sixty-three kilometres farther on.

For those who want to cling to the coast, however, Highway 219 follows the shore from Margaree Harbour to the Scottish town of Inverness, passing through communities with such Scottish names as Dunvegan, Kinloch, and Glenora, the site of the only distillery in Canada to produce Scottish-style single malt whisky. Here, the traveller may toast their visit to one of North America's most renowned scenic routes, the Cabot Trail.

The Cabot Trail and the Cape Breton Highlands National Park have both been ranked number one in Canada by 10Best.com, a travel website.

Trio of people wearing masks and costumes outside the Centre de la Mi-Carême in Chéticamp, Nova Scotia. An old Acadian tradition, the mid-Lent Masque et Mer de la Mi-Carême festival involves music, dancing, and the wearing of costumes and masks.

THIRTY

FROM SEA TO SKY AND BEYOND

The "Sea to Sky" Highway was a brand devised by the government of British Columbia to help attract and promote the 2010 Winter Olympics. And it worked. By the time the flame was lit by Wayne Gretzky, British Columbia had a brand-new four-lane highway leading along the spectacular Pacific coastline from Vancouver to the winter paradise of Whistler.

Today also known as Highway 99, the scenery doesn't just end at Whistler; it extends along the entire route, through rugged mountain passes, along blue-water lakes, and up the stunning Fraser Canyon gorge into Canada's driest desert region.

The starting point for this adventure begins in Vancouver's Stanley Park, a Canadian National Historic Site.

Made up of a four-hundred-hectare rainforest, the park includes First Nations heritage, trails, war-time remnants, and one of the world's most acclaimed seawalls.

Originally home to the Tsleil-Waututh and Musqueam Nations, it developed into a fishing colony and sawmill site. As the Canadian Pacific Railway was busy extending its rails into Vancouver, the railway company put in a request to the Canadian government for the land that the park now occupies. In 1886 the city council had other ideas and designated the forest as a park, naming it in honour of Lord Stanley, Canada's then governor general.

The first roads through the park followed early Indigenous trails and were covered with clam shells. Nonetheless, by 1909 the park was attracting thirty-three thousand visitors a year.

In 1924, to celebrate the area's First Nations heritage, totems from Haida Gwaii and Alert Bay were erected in the park. But the site remained subject to the whims of nature, such as in 1962 when Hurricane Freda destroyed three thousand trees, or in 1991 when a fierce winter storm levelled another two thousand, or in the winter blast of 2006, when ten thousand trees representing 10 percent of the forest were wrecked. However, the damage did not deter *Travel and Leisure* magazine in 2013 from declaring this remarkable urban oasis "one of the world's most beautiful parks."

From the park, Highway 99 makes its way across the iconic (and congested) Lions Gate Bridge, after which it briefly links up with the Trans-Canada Highway and makes its way to Horseshoe Bay, where the TCH heads for the ferry docks, destined for Vancouver Island. Meanwhile, the Sea to Sky Highway follows the mountainous coast.

A side trip before leaving Vancouver entirely is to Lighthouse Park, another National Historic Site, with a seventy-four-hectare virgin coastal rainforest.

The coastal journey hugs the seacoast, while cliffs rising as high as five hundred metres loom overhead. At Squamish, now a busy marine terminal, the Stawamus Chief, a sheer five-hundred-metre rock cliff, has become one of the world's most prized rock climbs.

Porteau Cove Provincial Park is situated on the Sea to Sky Highway in British Columbia. It lies on the most southerly fjord in North America. The waters off its coast, filled with shipwrecks and a wide array of marine life, attract many scuba divers.

Prior to the 1960s, there was no road here from Vancouver, and before the 1950s, not even a rail line. But today the shoreline offers up a number of stunning roadside attractions. The views from Porteau Cove are among the favourites, while foaming sheer waterfalls, such as the 335-metre Shannon Falls and the 70-metre Brandywine Falls, plunge from their mountain heights.

And there are even a couple of ghost towns.

At Britannia Beach, soaring nine storeys above the road, is the Britannia Mine mill building. Another National Historic Site, this copper mine, which operated from 1900 to 1974, was the largest in the British Empire. With its 210 kilometres of tunnels and large open pit, the mine employed 1,400 workers living in two townsites. High atop the mountain was the townsite of Mount Sheer, now reduced to mere rubble, while by the beach, the townsite of Britannia Beach remains largely intact. It sits right beside the highway. Most of the structures have been repurposed, and the soaring mill building has become a mining museum.

From the mine, the highway continues to Squamish. In 1912 Squamish began its rise with the building of the Pacific Great Eastern Railway from the port to Lillooet and then on to Williams Lake, where construction halted for several years due to difficulties in getting through the canyons north of that location.

Finally, in the 1950s, the rails made it through to Prince George and southward to Vancouver itself. It then became the British Columbia Railway, known worldwide for its popular dinner train hauled by the iconic Royal Hudson steam locomotive. BC Rail was subsequently bought by the CNR, known for its dislike of passenger trains, and so rail passenger service was ended, not just to Squamish but also to Prince George. Today the Royal Hudson rests forever silent in the West Coast Railway Museum in Squamish.

From Squamish to Whistler, Highway 99 swings inland and through the mountains to the site of one of the world's premier ski resorts, Whistler Blackcomb. Tourism here started modestly enough in 1910 when Alex and Myrtle Philip opened a fishing lodge on the shores of Alta Lake. When the Pacific Great Eastern Railway made its way in from Squamish in 1914, their Rainbow Lodge grew to accommodate a hundred guests and was the largest lodge west of Banff. The popularity and beauty of the location began to attract skiers, and several more lodges opened.

In fact, so popular had the region become that promoters, inspired by the success of the 1960 Squaw Valley Olympics, began to tout the site for the 1976 Olympics. But that dream would have to wait another thirty-five years. Nonetheless, the B.C. government established the municipality of Whistler in 1976, with land set aside for a new town centre. By 1992 Whistler Blackcomb was being called the "number one ski resort in North America," so there was little argument when it, along with the city of Vancouver, won the competition for the 2010 Winter Olympics. To help seal the bid, the B.C. government widened and straightened the highway and branded it the Sea to Sky Highway. Prior to that, the highway had been a winding two-lane route to Pemberton, which in itself was a vast improvement over the cattle trail that existed before 1964.

Today the town resembles a typical ski resort with upscale shops and Bavarian-style architecture. With gondola rides to the lofty peaks, Whistler is as busy in the summer as it is in the snowy winter. The Rocky Mountaineer's new Whistler railway station is situated in the new upscale Nita Lake Lodge on Lake Placid Road. The train tour is part of its three-day Rainforest to Gold Rush excursion from Vancouver to Jasper.

As for that first lodge in Whistler, the Rainbow Lodge on Alta Lake finally closed its doors in 1977 and now lies in Rainbow Park on the north shore of Alta Lake.

The Sea to Sky Highway ends at Whistler, while Highway 99 continues to Pemberton as a two-lane roadway. After a short twenty-two-kilometre drive, the route escapes from the mountain passes and into the lush flatlands of the Lillooet River.

Getting to Pemberton was never easy. At first, travellers had to journey along the Lillooet River to the head of Anderson Lake and Port Douglas, and then via Lillooet Lake to Mount Currie, the future site of Pemberton. In 1914 the rails of the Pacific Great Eastern Railway were completed from Squamish, and a new community of Pemberton developed around the station.

With its reputation for producing virus-free potatoes, the Pemberton region began to boom. Today, in keeping with that rural theme, the streets of the town have been given an Old West feel, with boom-town storefronts and covered sidewalks. Movie producers occasionally use the streets for their "Western" movie shoots.

The train station is a new structure with a traditional station style. Trains no longer pause here, however. The station hotel, now refurbished, still lies behind the station. The local museum offers displays of early farm and railway items.

From Pemberton's fertile valley, it's back into the mountains and one of British Columbia's least known yet most stunning mountain routes. From the shores of Lillooet Lake, Highway 99 climbs into the soaring mountains, where switchbacks carved into the steep mountain slopes recall earlier times, when the link between Mount Currie and the goldfields of the Fraser Valley was fraught with peril and dizzying drops.

After nearly one hundred kilometres, Highway 99 emerges from the valley of the Cayoosh Creek to meet the rushing Fraser River and the one-time gold rush boom town of Lillooet. As the 1858 gold rush into the Fraser Valley moved north from Yale, Lillooet boomed into a town of sixteen thousand, with thirteen saloons and thirty-five other licensed premises. After the gold rush faded, and prospectors moved on to the Cariboo goldfields, the town faded as well. It was revitalized with the arrival of the railway and its selection as a railway divisional point.

Today it has become the centre of a cattle-ranching area and is the junction of Highway 99 with Highway 12. The new station is quieter now with the ending of railway passenger service and today sees only visits from the two coaches of the Kaoham Shuttle, which brings passengers from the communities of Seton Portage and Shalalth. The little train, however, is gaining in popularity with tourists for its scenic shoreline route along the mountainous shores of Seton Lake.

Travel along the Cariboo Road has become much easier today and is now known as British Columbia's Highway 99.

While Lillooet serves primarily the local populations, it promotes its golden heritage with its sixteen historic plaques on its Golden Mile of History. A number of the commercial buildings along the main street reflect the boom town–style of its earlier heydays.

From Lillooet, Highway 99 leaves behind the mist-covered peaks and follows the gorge carved out by the Fraser River northward. Not always evident from the road, the deep gorge is tantalizingly just out of sight until one of the few lookout points along the route betrays the yawning chasm of the hurtling river.

At Pavilion, the highway turns eastward away from the river gorge and the original route of the Cariboo Road, which continued north to follow the Fraser from this point. As the highway makes its way over the rolling hills leading to Cache Creek, the land gets increasingly drier until at Highway 97 the land has become a dry grassland and desert, one of Canada's driest regions.

At the junction of the two highways stands a historic site that recalls the days of the gold rush, the Hat Creek Ranch. Built as a roadhouse in the 1880s for prospectors making their way to the Cariboo gold-fields, it later became a cattle ranch, and in 1977 a historic site. Here, costumed interpreters relay the hardships of those early days. The grounds include a general store, a blacksmith shop, gold panning, and a fully restored BC Express stagecoach, which visitors can ride. On display is one of western Canada's most extensive collections of farm equipment.

From Highway 99, Highway 97 leads a few kilometres south to the village of Cache Creek and its junction with the Trans-Canada Highway, and north to Quesnel and the goldfields of Cariboo country, where the golden boom town of Barkerville is now a restored ghost town.

THIRTY-ONE

SASQUATCH AND OTHER WANDERING WONDERS

Unlike canyons, mountains, and historic sites, not all Canada's wonders sit still. Some may be there one week for all to see and the next week gone. They are Canada's world-renowned wildlife wonders.

Perhaps the best known and most visited are the polar bears of Churchill, Manitoba. Thanks to its population of the massive white beasts, the remote Manitoba port has developed a lucrative tourist industry around polar bear viewing.

Churchill dates to the days of the Hudson's Bay Company, which established a fur-trading post in 1717, and the Prince of Wales Fort, begun in 1731, to protect it. In the early years of the twentieth century, various governments in western Canada urged the building of a rail link to Hudson Bay to compete with the monopolistic CPR. However, no rails arrived until 1929, when what is known today as the Hudson Bay Railway operated by the American rail giant OmniTRAX started service.

In the 1980s the local government began to promote the town as a destination for polar bear watching. Thanks to the rail link, tourists began to arrive in large numbers. Once there, they climb into the high "tundra buggies" well out of reach of the polar beast, which, when standing, can reach a height of more than three metres. Today Churchill is known as the polar bear capital of the world. Of the nineteen polar bear populations in the world, Canada can claim thirteen, the most accessible being that in Churchill.

In Canada, polar bears can be found from James Bay to northern Ellesmere Island and from Labrador to the Alaskan border. Churchill, Manitoba, on the western coast of Hudson Bay, is one of the three largest polar bear maternity denning areas in the world.

However, that opportunity may not last, as the polar bear population around Churchill is predicted to fall below seven hundred, or about half of what it was in 1984. Blame global warming, which is shrinking the sea ice where the bears catch their prey, the seal. Other research suggests that bear populations are remaining steady in other more northerly areas, such as Davis Strait and the Foxe Basin.

In 1970 the province of Ontario established Polar Bear Provincial Park on the shore of Hudson Bay. At more than 2.3 million hectares, it is Ontario's largest park and is home to a population of about two hundred bears. Access is by air only, and the park has no facilities.

Polar bears are an iconic symbol of northern Canada.

In far northeastern Ontario, the Cochrane Polar Bear Habitat is both the largest and the only human-care facility in the world dedicated solely to polar bears. With seven hectares of subarctic environment, the habitat also features the world's largest enclosed lake, which provides an ice platform for up to seven months of the year. While tourism is encouraged, the facility is foremost a bear habitat, and unless a visitor arrives at feeding time, the bears may remain out of sight. If they are lucky, children may be able to "swim" with the bears in a pool — divided, of course, by a solid glass barrier.

Polar bears, however, are not Canada's only white-coated bears. Lurking in the Great Bear Rainforest of British Columbia is an even rarer species, the Kermode bear. Its white coat is a genetic mutation of the normally black-coated black bear. So rare is the animal that its habitat locations are kept secret, although lodges in the rainforest will take tourists to those locations. Of the more than four hundred individuals in the rainforest, about one-quarter are protected in the Spirit Bear Conservancy.

While black bears and grizzlies roam through the country, nowhere on earth do three species coexist on one single island. Yet, on Herschel Island in the Beaufort Sea, black, grizzly, and polar bears are found together.

Canada's Arctic is also home to other world-renowned animal populations. For generations, Inuit across the region have depended on the massive migrating caribou herds for food and clothing. Herds numbering upward of 750,000 move en masse across the barrens of Nunavut. Others inhabit northern Quebec. Caribou-viewing excursions emanate from barren land communities like Baker Lake, Chesterfield Inlet, and Repulse Bay.

Meanwhile, in Ontario and Quebec, the woodland caribou roam in smaller herds, inhabiting more forested regions. A small herd on Michipicoten Island in Lake Superior coexists precariously with the resident wolf population.

Caribou, despite their distinctly Canadian pedigree, are among the world's most threatened species; they are adversely affected by global warming as well as loss of habitat and disruption to migration routes from mining and infrastructure building. Indeed, some herds in Canada have declined by as much as 90 percent.

Canada's North is also home to the strange-looking shaggy muskoxen. These members of the cattle family are found naturally only in the Canadian tundra and Arctic islands. Living in small herds, they are noted for their defensive mechanism of lining up in a tight formation to confront their attackers. Threatened by overhunting in the early years of the twentieth century, a ban on their killing from 1917 to 1970 saved them from extinction, as did the establishment of Thelon Wildlife Sanctuary in the Northwest Territories in 1927. The territory of Nunavut counts nearly sixty thousand muskoxen, many of which can be seen in the areas of Cambridge Bay, Gjoa Haven, and Grise Fiord, where various tour operators take tourists to see the hairy herds.

Until the 1850s Canada's prairies were home to more than forty million other hairy beasts, the buffalo. For thousands of years, they provided Indigenous inhabitants with their many needs: meat, clothing, fuel, and utensils. The arrival of the European hunters followed by railway in 1886 brought hordes of hunters, who, simply for the sport of it, shot any buffalo they could see, leaving the carcasses to rot where they fell. Farmers and ranchers soon followed, wiping out what little habitat remained. By 1900 fewer than a thousand of the animals remained.

Then the federal government realized it had precious little time to save what animals still survived and in 1909 created Buffalo National Park in Wainwright, Alberta. The initial herd of 325 plains buffalo quickly grew and by 1916 numbered 2,000 animals, making it the world's largest buffalo herd at the time. The herd, however, became too large for the Parks Service to manage at that location. Between 1925 and 1928, 6,673 of the plains buffalo were transported to the new Wood Buffalo National Park in northern Alberta. Here, the plains bison mingled with the wood bison, leading to an outbreak of debilitating diseases, like tuberculosis and brucellosis. In 1939 the government closed Buffalo National Park, turning the land over to the military.

Another sanctuary was created in 1913: the Elk Island National Park in northern Alberta. Although originally established as a preserve for the vanishing elk herds, it is recognized today as one of the world's pre-eminent elk and bison conservation reserves, providing habitat for six hundred plains and wood buffalo. The park measures 194 square kilometres and is Canada's only fully fenced park.

Less than a decade later, the government created the forty-five-thousand-square-kilometre Wood Buffalo National Park, home now to the world's last free-roaming wood bison herds. From the main visitor centre in Fort Smith, roads lead through the vast park, with frequent pull-overs to watch the buffalo herds as well as the endangered whooping cranes in the Whooping Crane Nesting Reserve in the north end of the park.

In 1983 UNESCO inscribed Wood Buffalo National Park as a World Heritage Site, citing it as "an outstanding example of ongoing ecological and biological processes encompassing some of the largest undisturbed grass and sedge meadows left in North America. It sustains the world's largest herd of wood bison, a threatened species."

While Canada's wolf population is not usually considered particularly rare, tourists arrive in droves to participate in Algonquin Park's nightly wolf howls. Led by park rangers expert in mimicking the howl of a wolf, the groups head out into the darkness, hoping that the rangers' howls will meet with a response.

Neither are Canada's moose that rare, although the unusual white moose population in the Foleyet region of northeastern Ontario might be an exception. Here, gene mutations have given a small population of the species their distinctive white lustre. Hunting them is prohibited.

Deer are ubiquitous across Canada and around much of the world, until one gets to Anticosti Island. Situated on the Gulf of St. Lawrence, it is one and a half times the size of Prince Edward Island but has a population of fewer than 250 people, and about 160,000 very friendly white-tail deer. It had long been a hunting ground for both Inuit and Mi'kmaq Peoples before being annexed by the French in the 1600s. It subsequently became British, and, following Confederation, became part of Quebec. With its extensive timber stands, a succession of timber companies moved in.

Then, in 1895, a wealthy French chocolate manufacturer named Henri Menier bought the entire island with the idea of turning it into his private hunting reserve and imported 220 white-tail deer. He opened a cannery and fish-packing plant and built the village of Port Menier to house his workers. Following his death in 1913, his brother sold the island to a logging company. Finally, in 1974, the government of Quebec bought the island, setting up a municipal government and creating a 572-square-kilometre conservation park. Today it is visited by nature lovers and hunters.

Anticosti is not the only east coast island with an unusual four-hoofed population. Sable Island is situated in the stormy Atlantic some 175 kilometres east of Nova Scotia. This forty-five-kilometre-long sliver of sand, although only a kilometre and a half across, is home to a rare population of 450 wild horses, a figure that fluctuates depending on annual mortality rates. How they got there is subject to some speculation, although the common theory is that they are descended from a group of sturdy Acadian horses brought there in the eighteenth century by a Boston merchant in a failed effort to establish a farming community. The horses live in small bands consisting of four to eight animals. There are an estimated forty such groups. They survive on the grasses that grow in the shifting dunes and by drinking pools of rainwater.

The herds were saved from removal in the 1960s by a letter-writing campaign launched by Canada's schoolchildren. As a result, the federal government in 1962 passed a law to protect the herd and in 2013

A stallion and his harem on Sable Island National Park Reserve. Although legend has it that these wild horses are the descendants of horses that survived the shipwrecks of sixteenth-century Portuguese explorers, the reality is that they were introduced to the island in the eighteenth century and eventually became feral.

established the Sable Island National Park Reserve. Parks Canada strictly regulates visits to the island.

Located off the coast of the Gaspé Peninsula in Quebec, the 4.16-square-kilometre Bonaventure Island is home to the world's largest bird sanctuary, created in 1919. Its 280,000 squawking denizens include 52,000 pairs of nesting gannets, the largest such colony on earth. In total, more than 280 species of avian critters make Bonaventure Island their home. Tour boats from the village of Percé circle the island to allow visitors to gape at the bird-filled crevices of its high cliffs.

Not all Canada's wildlife enjoy widespread appeal. For those who really want to, visitors to the Salt River Day-Use Area in Wood Buffalo National Park may watch the slithering mass of red-sided garter snakes disentangle themselves from their winter sleep each May and engage in a mass mating ritual before wriggling off across the grasslands for the summer.

The more widely known snake pit, however, is that in Narcisse, Manitoba. Here, for two brief periods each year, tens of thousands of red-sided garter snakes congregate at the surface of their winter dens, beginning with the first few warm days of spring. Then they, too, perform a mating ritual before dispersing to nearby marshes for the summer. By early fall, the harmless little serpents return to their dens, wintering in fissures and crevices of the limestone bedrock below the frozen ground. The Narcisse site is managed by the Wildlife Branch of the province of Manitoba, which provides parking, picnic sites, and washrooms. It is the largest such mass gathering of snakes in the world, and the province is happy to promote it.

Neither do the lowly squirrels garner much respect, but a rare population of white squirrels has become the iconic logo of the small community of Exeter, Ontario. Here, too, a genetic mutation in a local population of grey squirrels has given rise to about 250 of the elusive white, furry critters.

Canada's waters, too, attract worldwide acclaim. While whale watching is now ubiquitous worldwide, Canada's ocean waters contain a few species of whale that are almost unique in the world. Here lurks the ghostly beluga whale, whose white form attracts tourists by the boatload. Popular viewing areas are Pond Inlet in the Arctic and in the St. Lawrence River near the mouth of the Saguenay River, with its outflow of rich nutrients. Sadly, the heavily polluted waters of the river are threatening the future of the animals.

Northern waters are home to not only the belugas but also the legendary narwhal, whose three-metre-long single tusk has over the centuries created the legends of mythical sea monsters that instilled fear in the world's early navigators. The purpose of the tusk puzzles biologists to this day. Travelling in pods of ten to twenty members, the whales' main viewing areas lie around Resolute and Pond Inlet.

And then there is the sasquatch. The name, derived from the Coast Salish and Tsimshian Peoples of the Pacific Coast, has long been part of the Indigenous oral history, which describes the creature as tall, hairy, and foul smelling, but so elusive that no sighting has yet been fully verified.

The first European encounter occurred in 1811 when Northwest Company surveyor David Thompson wrote of finding footprints in the soil measuring fourteen inches long. Later, prospectors returning from the Klondike gold rush told of the ape men, but also of strange lights and woolly mammoths, yarns that were generally discounted.

One of the more elaborate tales was that recounted by one Albert Ostman, a B.C. logger who set off in 1924 to seek out a lost gold mine. Only in 1957 did he reveal that he had, in fact, been abducted by a large, hairy creature and held in a cave for six days with what he described as a sasquatch family before he made his escape.

Another abduction account was that of Muchalat Harry, a Nuu'chah'nult hunter who in 1928 was snatched while in his sleeping bag by a large sasquatch who carried him to what he claimed was a sasquatch camp. After a time, the creatures left, and Harry hurried back to his village.

Such tales, though, are rare. Most "encounters" usually consist of coming across huge footprints, strong foul odors, or strange sounds in the forests. These anecdotes have been told in Manitoba, Alberta, and as far east as Ontario. The sasquatch, like its cousins the yeti in Nepal, the yowie of Australia, and the yeren of China, may be little more than oral history descended from ancient memories of now-extinct hominid species such as the Neanderthal. Still, it all makes one wonder.

In 2012, the Assiniboine Zoo in Winnipeg opened its Polar Bear Conservation Centre. Here, orphaned bear cubs from the Churchill area are rehabilitated and then transitioned to the vast Journey to Churchill exhibit, which replicates their natural environment around Churchill, the world's polar bear capital. Now renamed the Leatherdale Polar Bear Conservation Centre, the exhibit, with its various arctic wildlife and terrain, is described as the "most comprehensive zoological exhibit of its kind in the world."

THIRTY-TWO

THE VIMY RIDGE MEMORIAL:
THE FINAL CHAPTER

In northern France there is a hundred-hectare patch of Canada. And on that patch, high atop a prominent ridge, rises a soaring limestone monument. One of the world's most stunning memorials, it is a tribute to the sixty-six thousand Canadian men who died on the battlefields of the First World War or who succumbed to their injuries afterward. It stands atop the very ridge where four Canadian battalions conquered the German trenches and achieved one of the most strategic victories of the war. It was a victory that neither the French nor the British could achieve in the months leading up to it. It was the Battle of Vimy Ridge.

Vimy Ridge is a seven-kilometre-long height of land overlooking an open plain to the north. It was on that plain that a hundred thousand French troops were killed or wounded in their repeated failed attempts to capture the strategic hill.

The four Canadian battalions, together for the first time and under the command of General Julian Byng, not only planned their assault in advance but also rehearsed it. Troops were assigned specific roles and practiced them using maps and models derived from aerial photographs. Another technique would be the use of rolling artillery fire. The great guns would unleash a barrage on the German lines for a week in advance to keep the enemy hiding in their dugouts while the troops crept forward through a network of secret tunnels.

Then, at 5:30 a.m. on April 9, 1917, 15,000 Canadians streamed out of the tunnels and, following the curtain of exploding shells, overtook the enemy lines. It took three days to totally secure the ridge, and in that time nearly 3,600 Canadians were killed and 7,000 wounded. But as Brigadier General A.E. Ross would later declare, "In those few minutes I witnessed the birth of a nation."

Vimy was not the only battle where the Canadians earned distinction. On April 22, 1915, while entrenched with other allies at the Second Battle of Ypres, Canadians held fast against a deadly onslaught of chlorine gas followed by a second two days later. By holding urine-soaked rags to their faces, the Canadians defied the gas attacks and held their ground long enough for British reservists to move into the action.

July 1916 witnessed one of the war's deadliest fights. Here, at the Battle of the Somme, a river near the village of Beaumont-Hamel, the Royal Newfoundland Regiment was virtually wiped out; only 68 of 801 Newfoundlanders survived the day. The proud citizens

The Vimy Memorial.

of Newfoundland and Labrador commemorate this act of gallantry each year on November 11. It is their Remembrance Day.

For the Canadians, however, the Battle of Passchendaele has been described by one of its survivors as "one of the bloodiest of the war."

It was October 1917 when British general Sir Douglas Haig, acting against the advice of Canadian corps commander General Arthur Currie, ordered 100,000 Canadians into battle. Slogging through knee-deep mud, the Canadians eventually won the field only to have the British evacuate it the following year. For their efforts, 15,600 Canadian soldiers were killed or wounded.

In August 1918, with the Armistice only three months away, the Battle of Amiens went much better, for here the Canadians used the element of surprise. Rather than alert the enemy with an advance barrage of artillery fire, the Canadians rushed suddenly toward the surprised Germans, and, along with tanks and aerial bombardment, overwhelmed the enemy lines, taking ten thousand prisoners and 165 artillery pieces before continuing beyond the lines for another thirteen kilometres, the greatest single Allied advance during the stalemated war.

Despite the Canadians' bravery and military achievements, many historians continue to wonder whether the war, with so many deaths and so little gained, was even worth it, especially since the restrictive terms of the peace treaty were believed to have later contributed to the start of the Second World War.

In 1922, in a fitting gesture of gratitude, the government of France ceded to Canada the very land on which the Canadians scored their victory, a hundred-hectare plot atop the Vimy Ridge.

Following the war, a Canadian Battlefields Memorial Commission was struck to decide on a location and memorial to commemorate the war dead; they issued an invitation for submissions for a fitting design. More than 160 entries came in. Rather than placing the winning design in all eight significant battlefields in which Canadians participated, the site chosen, at the urging of Prime Minister Mackenzie King, was the Canadian land at Vimy.

The final design choice was that submitted by Walter Allward. His work was already well regarded, including a monument to the Northwest Rebellion in 1896 and to the Boer War in 1910, both located in Toronto.

Allward was most concerned about the material to be used for the memorial. After considerable searching, he selected a disused third-century limestone quarry in Yugoslavia that had been used to construct the ancient palace of Diocletian.

The base of his giant piece measures eleven metres high and thirty-seven metres deep, upon which soar a pair of vertical columns thirty metres high. Clustered around the memorial stand twenty sculpture figures that bear names like Truth, Justice, the Defenders, Hope, and Faith. The most prominent and poignant of the figures is Canada Bereft, a woman with head bowed clutching wilting flowers, intended to honour the grieving mothers of their fallen sons.

Around the base itself are inscribed the names of the more than eighteen thousand fallen soldiers with no known graves. Upon witnessing the work, Group of Seven artist A.Y. Jackson declared that there would never be another like it.

When King Edward VIII unveiled the memorial in 1936, he described Vimy as representing a coming of age for Canada.

In addition to the massive sculpture itself, the Canadian government has preserved the grounds and has retained the tunnels that hid not only the Canadian troops but also the German defenders.

During the Second World War, the memorial received an unlikely visitor in Adolf Hitler, who was apparently sufficiently impressed with the memorial that he ordered it not to be destroyed.

Refurbishments occurred in 2005 and 2006. Today visitors can still see the hundreds of bomb craters that pockmark the off-limit grounds and tour

Although these trenches look pleasant today, during the Battle of Vimy Ridge, they were poisonous, muddy traps, filled with dead soldiers, rats, unexploded grenades, and overwhelming amounts of cold, swampy mud.

the labyrinth of tunnels, many of which contain artifacts of the battlefields and inscriptions left by the troops themselves.

On April 9, 2017, as part of a poignant centennial tribute to the sacrifices at Vimy, a new visitor centre opened, containing the story of the memorial, letters from soldiers, artifacts, and a panoramic view of the massive field of shell craters.

The view from the memorial over the plains below underscores the daunting challenge that faced the Canadian battalions in their gritty and deadly struggle to overcome the German guns and trenches. The distinctive stone memorial is one of Canada's most significant memorials and one of the grandest war memorials in the world; for the thousands who sacrificed their lives, it is their "final chapter."

ACKNOWLEDGEMENTS

A work of this nature requires input from countless individuals and agencies. While an amazing amount of material is available online, thanks to the many dedicated historical societies and agencies, nothing matches the personal contacts who have first-hand experiences with the many and varied "wonders" that Canada shares with the world at large.

First and foremost is Parks Canada. Thanks to Guy Theriault, senior marketing specialist, this agency has offered advice, literature, and images that Parks Canada researchers and staff have accumulated over several years. A special shout-out goes to Professor Jean-Michel Gastonguay of the Observatoire de l'Astroblème de Charlevoix for a first-hand tour of the strange geological manifestations of one of Canada's most significant meteor impacts.

Tourism agencies, notably Tourisme Québec, Tourisme Charlevoix, Cape Breton Tourism, and Thousand Islands Tourism, have provided important assistance and vital insight into the incredible regions they cover. Yukon Tourism also shared information on their storied land. Amanda Pausner of Grey County Tourism not only assisted me but also introduced me to Ron Savage, author of a book on Silent Valley, who led me through the forested paths and introduced me to the secrets of this tranquil oasis.

I am happy to acknowledge the curators and staff at Minister's Island and at the grand Canadian Pacific Railway station in Macadam, both in New Brunswick, for their personalized and highly informative tours, as well as the knowledgeable staff at Dinosaur Provincial Park in Alberta. Also a special shout-out goes to Erik Lamberston of the Royal B.C. Museum in Victoria for his important consultation on the remarkable collection of totem poles showcased by that renowned institution.

Finally, I want to acknowledge my close friend Gordon Wagar, now deceased, who, over many years, offered me the opportunity to explore and learn about the Thirty Thousand Islands of Georgian Bay, our favourite stomping ground.

IMAGE CREDITS

INDEX

BOOK CREDITS

Acquiring Editor: Margaret Bryant
Developmental Editor: Dominic Farrell
Project Editor: Jenny McWha
Copy Editor: Melissa Churchill
Proofreader: Tara Quigley

Cover Designer: Laura Boyle
Interior Designer: Jennifer Gallinger

Publicist: Elham Ali

DUNDURN

Publisher: J. Kirk Howard
Vice-President: Carl A. Brand
Editorial Director: Kathryn Lane
Artistic Director: Laura Boyle
Director of Sales and Marketing: Synora Van Drine
Publicity Manager: Michelle Melski

Editorial: Allison Hirst, Dominic Farrell, Jenny McWha, Rachel Spence, Elena Radic
Marketing and Publicity: Kendra Martin, Kathryn Bassett, Elham Ali

dundurn.com   dundurnpress
@dundurnpress   dundurnpress
dundurnpress   info@dundurn.com

FIND US ON NETGALLEY & GOODREADS TOO!

DUNDURN